Didactics of Physical Education and Sport

Nils Neuber

Didactics of Physical Education and Sport

Foundations and Models

 Springer

Nils Neuber
Universität Münster
Münster, Germany

ISBN 978-3-658-47187-3   ISBN 978-3-658-47188-0   (eBook)
https://doi.org/10.1007/978-3-658-47188-0

Translation from the German language edition: "Fachdidaktik Sport" by Nils Neuber, © Der/
die Herausgeber bzw. der/die Autor(en), exklusiv lizenziert an Springer Fachmedien Wiesbaden
GmbH, ein Teil von Springer Nature 2023. Published by Springer Fachmedien Wiesbaden. All
Rights Reserved.

This book is a translation of the original German edition "Fachdidaktik Sport" by Nils Neuber,
published by Springer Fachmedien Wiesbaden GmbH in 2023. The translation was done with the
help of an artificial intelligence machine translation tool. A subsequent human revision was done
primarily in terms of content, so that the book will read stylistically differently from a conven-
tional translation. Springer Nature works continuously to further the development of tools for the
production of books and on the related technologies to support the authors.

This Springer imprint is published by the registered company Springer Fachmedien Wiesbaden
GmbH, part of Springer Nature.
The registered company address is: Abraham-Lincoln-Str. 46, 65189 Wiesbaden, Germany

If disposing of this product, please recycle the paper.

Acknowledgment

Firstly, I would like to thank our students in the Master of Education program for their support in the development of this textbook, who have subjected the contents of the volume to a permanent practical test with their critical inquiries in the lecture "Didactic Concepts in Physical Education and Sport". Clarissa Lamm, Tim Becker, Nele Welling, and Frederike Kersten assisted me with all questions of text research and compiled the bibliographies. Tim Becker, Philipp Ciupke, Frederike Kersten, and Nils Kaufmann demonstrated patience and expertise in the design of the illustrations. Collegial feedback came from Kathrin Aschebrock, Ahmet Derecik, Franziska Duensing-Knop, Marion Golenia, Nils Kaufmann, Uta Kaundinya, Andre Magner, Michael Pfitzner, Esther Pürgstaller, Sebastian Salomon, and especially from Kathrin Kohake, who read everything. Kathrin Aschebrock took over the final editing and perfected the citation standard. The translation into Englisch was checked by Stefanie Dahl, Anabelle, Krüger, Renate Nocon-Stoffers and Andre Magner. And my wife Frauke Neuber has always supported me or strengthened me, depending on what was needed at the time. I sincerely thank all of them for their active support.

Münster   Nils Neuber
in March 2025

Contents

List of Tables

Introduction

1

Sport has developed into a significant societal phenomenon in the second half of the 20th century. Children's and youth sports, leisure and mass sports, performance and competitive sports, adventure and trend sports, health and senior sports, etc.—the **forms of sports** are almost unlimited. At the same time, the "idea of sport" permeates wide societal areas such as leisure, education, health, economic, or media systems. Sport is thus "more than the sum of sports, sports activities, and sports opportunities. Sport has become a part of the everyday life of many people" (Grupe and Krüger 2007, p. 69). In the course of the **differentiation of sports**, it has, however, experienced a tremendous increase in complexity, which is expressed in an increasing delimitation of the traditional concept of sport. Sport can serve performance enhancement, making contact, self-presentation, body shaping, relaxation, health promotion, etc. In the present case, it is interpreted with pedagogical intent. The focus is particularly on the **promotion of children and adolescents** through movement, games, and sports activities.

Movement and sport are among the most common and important activities in the **growing up of children and adolescents.** Already in preschool age, most girls and boys regularly participate in movement offers in daycare centers or sports clubs. In primary school age, the binding rates of sports clubs sometimes increase to over 80% of an age cohort, and almost all adolescents regularly practice at least one sport in their youth (cf. Züchner 2013). Therefore, sports can be confidently referred to as a **youth-specific age norm** (Zinnecker 1991). However, movement, games, and sports activities are not inherently pedagogically significant. Their pedagogical effect depends on the one hand on the conditions under which they take place. Different **learning locations** offer different formal, non-formal, and informal learning and educational potentials, which can be used differently by adolescents (see Sect. 3.3.4). On the other hand, the pedagogical

N. Neuber, *Didactics of Physical Education and Sport*,
https://doi.org/10.1007/978-3-658-47188-0_1

effect of sports offers is significantly dependent on their **pedagogical staging**, i.e., the way they are designed.

In this respect, sports didactic works is usually oriented towards the dual objective of an **education for sport**s and an **education through sports** (cf. Scherler 1997). On this basis, Beckers (2001) also justifies two **tasks of pedagogical action in sport** (see Fig. 1.1):

▶ **Education ("Erziehung")** Starting from the demands of society, education aims at structuring thinking, feeling, and acting. In relation to the field of sports, this means the transmission of skills and abilities, attitudes, and knowledge that one needs for practicing sports in a society.

▶ **Formation ("Bildung")** on the other hand, starts from the individual possibilities and desires of the individual and aims at the life design of the subject. In relation to sport, this means that the individual is put in a position to find their way in the diversity of sports offers, to develop their own standpoint, and to integrate sport meaningfully into their everyday life.

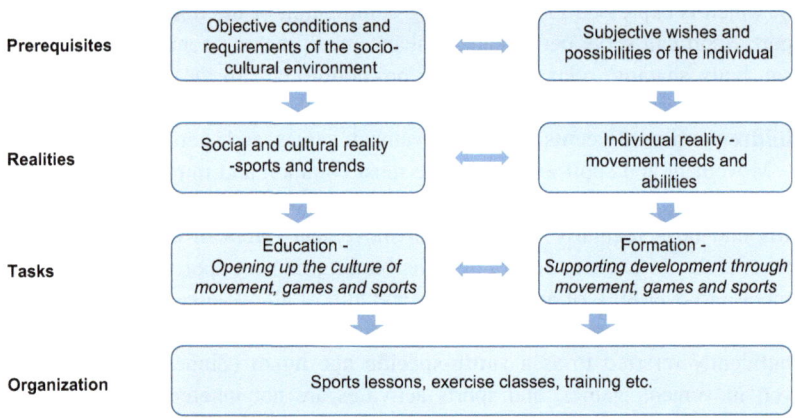

Fig. 1.1 Taks: Education – Opening up the culture of movement, games and sport Formation – Promoting development through movement, games and sport (Mod. according to Beckers 2001, p. 30)

Both aspects of pedagogical action can only be thought of in mutual interlocking: "While education is directed towards the **matter** and thereby conveys 'patterns of formed behavior', formation aims at the **person** and their ability for self-design, which includes the self-determined handling of these patterns" (Beckers 2001, p. 34).

▶ **Dual mandate of school sports** The two tasks of pedagogical action form the basis for the dual mandate of school sports: Exploration of movement, games, and sports culture as well as development promotion through movement, play, and sport (MSW NRW 2014).

The mandate is associated with principles of an **educational physical education ("Erziehender Sportunterricht"),** such as those of multiperspectivity, experience and action orientation, reflection, understanding or value orientation (MSWWF NRW 1999). With this explicitly pedagogical perspective on sports, school sports can make a specific contribution to the general **educational and teaching mission of the school**. Accordingly, in addition to subject-specific goals, contributions of school sports to cross-curricular tasks of the school are mentioned, e.g. traffic education, health promotion, intercultural education, political education, aesthetic education or reflective coeducation (MSWWF NRW 1999). Also, **extracurricular educational and teaching concepts** in sports refer to the idea of a dual mandate of pedagogical action (cf. Neuber 2018). Without being able to delve deeper into this pedagogical argumentation at this point, this outlines the basis for the **promotion of children and adolescents** in and through movement, games and sports (see Sect. 3.3).

The question remains as to what competencies teachers in the school and extracurricular field need in order to be able to act in this supportive way. To describe the competencies, a **dimensional competence model** has proven to be effective, which is based on the "Model of Teacher Development" by Terhart (2007) (see Fig. 1.2). According to this, the competence of teachers develops from the interaction of cognitive, moral and practical dimensions (Terhart 2007, pp. 49–50). The first dimension refers to the **knowledge** they need about school and teaching, teachers and learners, in order to be able to act successfully. The second dimension concerns the attitudes and **stances,** the pedagogical self-understanding, which is necessary for pedagogical action in PE. The third dimension refers to the didactic **action** or more modestly: the ability of "didacticizing", i.e. the ability to think didactically (cf. Neuber 2016). The

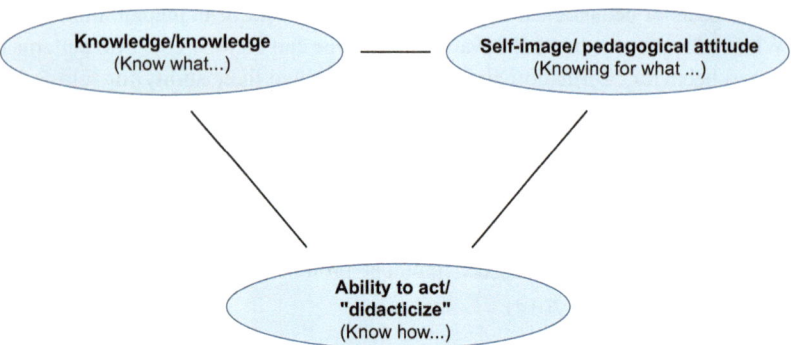

Fig. 1.2 Dimensional competence model of PE teacher education. (Mod. according to Terhart 2007, p. 50)

three-dimensional basic structure of the model can, if necessary, be related to sub-competencies, such as the subject, self or social competence of teachers (cf. Miethling and Gieß-Stüber 2007).

The competence model refers to central dimensions of the **qualification of physical education teachers.** Initially, it is irrelevant whether they are students, trainee teachers, or teachers in the profession. These dimensions are also of fundamental importance in the non-school sector, for example in the training of coaches in clubs (Golenia and Neuber 2014). The crucial point is that the model addresses essential **aspects of pedagogical action in sports** that should be addressed in the qualification of teachers. In this sense, the dimensional competence model is also the basis for the present textbook "Didactics of Physical Education and Sport – Foundations and Models", which accordingly pursues three central **objectives**:

- Firstly, **basic knowledge** about sociocultural conditions and pedagogical foundations, didactic models and concepts, as well as methodological basics and the concept of individual promotion should be conveyed. The focus here is primarily on overarching considerations and concepts for describing the prerequisites and structures of physical education.
- Furthermore, by presenting central prerequisites of physical education as well as selected didactic models, conceptions, and methods, the readers should gain an overview of the spectrum of action in general terms. Ultimately, this should provide the opportunity to adopt and justify an **educational self-understanding** and an *own* didactic position.

- Finally, the textbook aims at the **practical thinking and action** of teachers in sports in the sense of a "didactic thinking ability". Starting from basic terms and principles, the chapters provide suggestions for staging physical education. These are supplemented by tips for further reading and thinking. Reflection questions conclude each chapter (see box).

The structure of the textbook follows a simple instructional-theoretical **basic model for physical education** (see Fig. 1.3). After the introduction, sociocultural conditions and pedagogical basics of physical education are outlined. The next chapters deal with didactic models and concepts. This is followed by considerations on methods in physical education and on individual promotion in sports as an integrative concept. Overall, the textbook thus aims at *general* prerequisites of physical education. This also includes that the selected concepts usually have a **wide range**, i.e., they refer to physical education as a whole (see Sect. 5.3). This is different in the two subsequent volumes on target groups and prerequisites (Neuber 2020) and on subject areas and perspectives (Neuber 2021). In these, *specific* aspects of physical education are discussed and didactic concepts of **medium range** are presented.

Specifically, one volume is dedicated to the **prerequisite fields** of the instructional-theoretical basic model (pupils, *teachers* and *school*). For this, there are chapters on children as a target group in sports, adolescents as a target group in sports, girls and boys as a target group in sports, heterogeneous target groups in

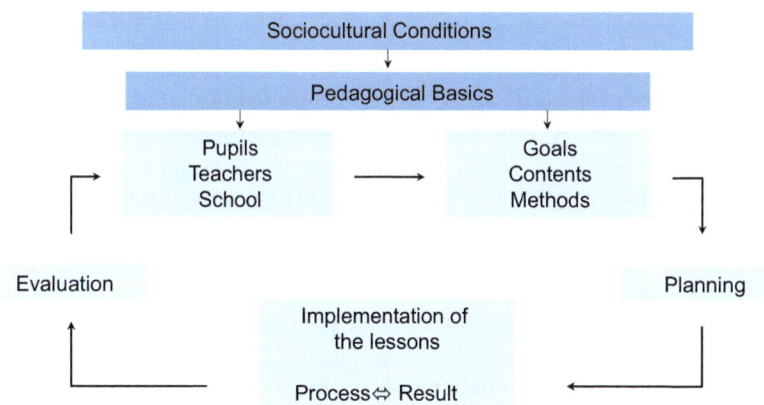

Fig. 1.3 Instructional-theoretical basic model of physical education. (Mod. according to Neuber 2000, p. 103)

sports, physical education teachers, and movement, play, and sports in school development (Neuber 2020). The other volume deals with the **decision fields** of the instructional-theoretical basic model (*goals, contents* and *methods*). This is done along the six pedagogical perspectives in chapters on perception and body experience, creative movement education, adventure and adventure sports, performance, achievement and success in sports, social learning in sports, and health promotion in sports (Neuber 2021). Practice-related **basics of physical education** in school (structural perspective), for planning, implementation, and evaluation of teaching sports (process perspective), as well as for the practical semester in sports will be addressed in further volumes.

The selection of the presented approaches and concepts is inevitably subjective. Therefore, the volumes are not about completeness, but about providing a **guidance** in the spectrum of didactic positions (Balz 2009), which allows the readers to develop their own standpoint. While the present volume is intended to provide a general, basic orientation for the broad field of **physical education and teaching sports**, the two subsequent volumes aim at specific aspects of the field. Sports didactics offer numerous medium-range approaches that address sub-areas of physical education, but have so far hardly been presented in an overview. Overall, this should provide the basis for study and teaching in the field of sports didactics. At the same time, a comparatively large **spectrum of pedagogical practice in sports** is depicted, which can be interesting not only for students, but also for pupils, trainee teachers, teachers, and pedagogical specialists in the extracurricular field.

Sections of the Textbook

The chapters of the textbook are always structured in the same way. For easier orientation, the same **structural features** are used:

- A **summary** provides an overview of the orientation and contents of the chapter in advance.
- The **introduction** outlines the importance of the topic and establishes the connection to the overall context of the textbook.
- Central **basic concepts** of a topic are presented in an overview at the beginning.
- Subsequently, the **foundations** of a topic are developed comprehensively but concisely and deepened in sub-aspects.

- In conclusion, the considerations are summarized once again in a **overview**.
- **Reflection questions** stimulate thought; they aim not only at the reproduction of knowledge, but also at stimulating the transfer into practice.
- Basic **definitions** are highlighted separately in the text.
- **Literature tips** supplement the text and are intended to encourage further reading.
- In addition, there is always a **knowledge module,** which offers a different, sometimes cross-cutting perspective on the topic of the chapter.

References

Balz, E. (2009). Fachdidaktische Konzepte update oder: Woran soll sich der Schulsport orientieren? *Sportpädagogik, 33*(1), 25–32.

Beckers, E. (2001). Sportpädagogik und Erziehungswissenschaft. In H. Haag & A. Hummel (Eds.), *Handbuch Sportpädagogik* (2., erweiterte Aufl., pp. 25–34). Schorndorf: Hofmann.

Golenia, M., & Neuber, N. (2014). *Empirische Untersuchung zu Kompetenzentwicklung und Einstellungsveränderungen bei Teilnehmerinnen und Teilnehmern der Übungsleiter-C-Ausbildung des Landessportbundes NRW* (Projektbericht). Münster: WWU.

Grupe, O., & Krüger, M. (2007). *Einführung in die Sportpädagogik* (3. neu bearbeitete Aufl.). Schorndorf: Hofmann.

Miethling, W.-D., & Gieß-Stüber, P. (2007). Persönlichkeit, Kompetenzen und Professionelles Selbst des Sport- und Bewegungslehrers. In W.-D. Miethling & P. Gieß-Stüber (Eds.), *Beruf: Sportlehrer/in* (pp. 1–24). Hohengehren: Schneider.

MSW NRW (Ministerium für Schule und Weiterbildung des Landes Nordrhein-Westfalen). (2014). *Rahmenvorgaben für den Schulsport in Nordrhein-Westfalen.* Düsseldorf: MSW.

MSWWF NRW (Ministerium für Schule und Weiterbildung, Wissenschaft und Forschung des Landes Nordrhein-Westfalen). (Eds.). (1999). *Richtlinien und Lehrpläne für die Sekundarstufe II – Gymnasium/Gesamtschule in Nordrhein-Westfalen. Sport.* Frechen: Ritterbach.

Neuber, N. (2000). *Kreativität und Bewegung – Grundlagen kreativer Bewegungserziehung und empirische Befunde* (Schriften der Deutschen Sporthochschule, 45). St. Augustin: Academia.

Neuber, N. (2016). Von der Theorie zur Praxis – und wieder zurück? Sportlehrerbildung als Forschungs- und Gestaltungsaufgabe. In D. Wiesche, M. Fahlenbock & N. Gissel (Eds.), *Sportpädagogische Praxis – Ansatzpunkt und Prüfstein von Theorie* (Schriften der Deutschen Vereinigung für Sportwissenschaft, 255, pp. 50–70). Hamburg: Czwalina.

Neuber, N. (2018). Sport und informelles Lernen. In T. Burger, M. Harring & M. Witte (Eds.), *Handbuch informelles Lernen – Interdisziplinäre und internationale Perspektiven* (2. edn., pp. 581–594). Weinheim, Basel: Beltz Juventa.

Neuber, N. (2020). *Fachdidaktische Konzepte Sport – Zielgruppen und Voraussetzungen* (Basiswissen Lernen im Sport). Wiesbaden: Springer VS. https://doi.org/10.1007/978-3-658-28464-0.

Neuber, N. (2021). *Fachdidaktische Konzepte Sport II – Themenfelder und Perspektiven* (Basiswissen Lernen im Sport). Wiesbaden: Springer VS. https://doi.org/10.1007/978-3-658-30249-8.

Scherler, K. (1997) Die Instrumentalisierung der Sportpädagogik. *Sportpädagogik, 21*(2), 5–11.

Terhart, E. (2007). Erfassung und Beurteilung der beruflichen Kompetenz von Lehrkräften. In M. Lüders & J. Wissinger (Eds.), *Forschung zur Lehrerbildung. Kompetenzentwicklung und Prorammevaluation* (pp. 37–62). Münster: Waxmann.

Zinnecker, J. (1991). Jugend als Bildungsmoratorium. In W. Melzer, W. Heitmeyer, L. Liegle & J. Zinnecker (Eds.), *Osteuropäische Jugend im Wandel* (pp. 9–25). Weinheim: Juventa.

Züchner, I. (2013). Sportliche Aktivitäten im Aufwachsen junger Menschen. In M. Grgic & I. Züchner (Eds.), *Medien, Kultur und Sport. Was Kinder und Jugendliche machen und ihnen wichtig ist. Die MediKuS-Studie* (pp. 89–138). Weinheim: Beltz Juventa.

Sociocultural Conditions

2

Abstract

This chapter deals with central sociocultural prerequisites for the growing up of children and adolescents. Starting from social change in modern societies, the growing up of children and adolescents, the living environments of children and adolescents, the change in the education system, as well as the importance of movement, games, and sport in municipal educational landscapes are presented. An excursion to the all-day school in municipal educational landscapes complements the chapter.

2.1 Introduction

Movement, games, and sports offerings for children and adolescents do not take place in a "vacuum," but always occur against the backdrop of a society's sociocultural conditions. On the one hand, this involves the social **significance of sports.** In modern societies, sports are "characterized by growth and differentiation. More and more people and groups of the population participate in the most diverse forms of sports—sometimes only through sportswear. The spread of sports at every age is not only reflected in the development of new sports and innovative forms of movement, but also in an overall expanded understanding of sports" (Güllich and Krüger 2022, p. 5). On the other hand, it is about the importance a society attaches to the **growing up of children and adolescents:** Should young people become adults as "smoothly" as possible, or are they allowed a more or less autonomous phase of trying out and experimenting (Reinders 2006)?

Ultimately, this is about the political **value of childhood, youth, and education** and the resources a society provides for it.

In this context, Größing (2007, p. 38) writes about **school sports:** "The economic and normative foundations and basic questions of a society and its education, social and sports policy significantly determine the value of school sports in the canon of subjects, how many hours per week are allocated to it, what the equipment of school sports facilities looks like and the training of sports teachers." The same applies to extracurricular **children's and youth sports,** whose importance is also largely dependent on the respective social and cultural attributions (cf. Neuber 2021a). In this respect, the **sociocultural conditions**—in addition to the "anthropogenic prerequisites" of the acting persons—are among the general conditioning factors of sports and (sports) teaching (Jank and Meyer 2020, pp. 262–264). The *anthropogenic* prerequisites, such as children or heterogeneous target groups, as well as the *specific* sociocultural prerequisites, such as the social construction of gender or the experience society, are presented elsewhere (Neuber 2020, 2021b). The following is about presenting the *general* sociocultural **prerequisites for growing up** of children and adolescents.

2.2   Basic Concepts

The term **social change** has been used since the mid-1980s to describe fundamental structural changes in society that have led to the overcoming of traditional values and patterns in post-war Germany. Since the 1990s, the term has been used to refer to modern or postmodern societies in the context of Western industrial or service nations. In this context, **individualization** means that the individual can increasingly less rely on classic family and work biographies and is thus increasingly responsible for his or her biography (cf. Beck 1986). **Pluralization** means that increasingly diverse value systems and life designs are possible, for which the individual must actively decide. These societal upheavals take place accelerated and temporally condensed, for which the term **dynamization** stands (cf. Rosa 2005). At the same time, these development processes are driven forward by new information and communication media in the course of **digitalization.**

Considering this background, the term **living environment** comes into focus when looking at the growing up of children and adolescents. This term describes the social and cultural conditions in which the everyday life of young people takes place, e.g., family, peer group, and leisure facilities (Größing 1993). Schools also have a social significance in this context. The term **institutionalization** expresses that adolescents spend more and more time in daycare and school and thus in "public responsibility" (cf. Rauschenbach 2015). At the center of this development is the all-day school, which is supposed to connect the different school and extracurricular **educational modalities** by combining both compulsory, certified and voluntary, unorganized learning. This goes hand in hand with the idea of the **educational landscape,** in which the various educational actors of a community are networked to best promote the individual educational biographies of the adolescents (Süßenbach 2021).

2.3 Foundations

The term **social change** describes long-term societal transformation processes, such as from the medieval estate society to the pluralistic society of modern times (Schubert and Klein 2022). In recent discussions, this term refers to the transition from the German post-war society to the modern or **postmodern society** of the 1990s and 2000s (see Fig. 2.1). Modern societies are characterized by increasing societal **differentiation**, which leads to a division of societal subsystems, such as the separation of work and leisure or education and religion. This is associated with a stronger role differentiation, which demands different, often new competencies from individuals (Tillmann 2010, pp. 316–351). At the same time,

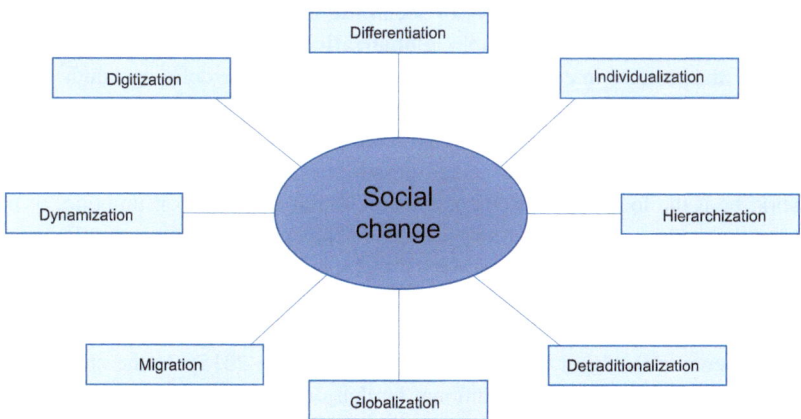

Fig. 2.1 Characteristics of social change in the second half of the 20th century. (Own illustration)

established forms of life are fading, which is referred to with the keyword **detraditionalization**. This means that "traditional patterns and models have lost their binding (social-controlling) function on the one hand, and their orienting (and thus relieving) function on the other" (Münchmeier 1998, p. 12). Detraditionalization leads to a release from traditional binding and control mechanisms and guarantees a stronger **pluralization** of possible life patterns. This not only brings a multitude of new, socially accepted forms of life (e.g., patchwork and rainbow families), but also a coexistence of various value systems in which the individual must locate themselves ("value pluralization").

This diversity offers the individual the opportunity to choose from a large number of options ("multi-option society"). On the other hand, it increases the pressure on the individual to take responsibility for their own life path.

▶ **Individualization** in this context means that the individual, detached from family traditions or societal classes, must make their own decisions. They must "learn to understand themselves as a center of action, as a planning office in relation to their life course, their abilities, orientations, partnerships, etc." (Beck 1986, p. 217). The responsibility for one's own biography thus lies with each individual themselves.

This also means the **end of the traditional normal biography.** Against the backdrop of destandardized life courses, the experience of risks and the possibility of failure become omnipresent (Hornstein 1997, pp. 24–25).

This fundamental restructuring of social life is continually driven forward by current developments. For example, **globalization** in the sense of political, economic, and cultural integration of the world is one of the defining trends at the beginning of the 21st century. Especially for young people, "the global horizon of a world society is more than ever a reality that significantly influences their thinking and actions, be it the gained possibilities of mobility and a global network, be it the local impressions of a multicultural world of consumption, or be it the ambivalent, crisis-ridden experiences of impending economic and financial crises or ecological disasters" (BMFSFJ 2013, p. 57). Closely linked to globalization is the **migration** of people who are drawn to other countries for various reasons. This leads on the one hand to an increase in cultural and ethnic diversity, which benefits the labor market (Mutz and Burrmann 2015). In the short term, however, it also leads to an additional burden on the education and social systems. The opportunities and risks of immigration became particularly clear during the so-called refugee crisis in 2015.

Another sociopolitical challenge is the **demographic change**. The population in Germany is shrinking, while at the same time becoming more diverse, colorful, and older. Added to this are regional differences between economically strong and weak regions, between metropolitan areas and large cities on the one hand and rural areas on the other, between regions with a high and low proportion of migrants (cf. Schmidt et al. 2015). The development of modern societies is characterized by an increasing acceleration, which leads to ever shorter half-lives of knowledge and certainties (Rosa 2005). In this sense, the **dynamization** of societal patterns and styles is one of the key terms of modernity. It is largely driven by the **digitalization** of society. This is less about technical knowledge and more about new ways of information and communication that naturally permeate the everyday life of the "Digital Natives", without them being able to draw on the experiences of difference of older generations. A life without digital media is unimaginable for them (BMFSFJ 2013, p. 55).

At the beginning of the 2020s, the **COVID-19 pandemic** added significant societal restrictions, which brought enormous challenges for young people in particular (Andresen et al. 2022). At the same time, social tensions intensified during this period. In part, these conflicts led to a rejection of the democratic constitutional state. Thus, ensuring **political participation** for all people is also one of the sociopolitical challenges of modernity (Vorländer 2013). Overall, the brief problem outline shows that modern societies have become more diverse and colorful, but also more ambivalent and risky due to the social transformation processes in the second half of the 20th century (cf. Beck 1986). Old certainties and values are being questioned, new trends and patterns often emerge at a high pace. Pedagogical action in general and **sports pedagogical action** in particular is repeatedly called upon to address current societal conditions. With a view to the central target group of children and adolescents, the **sociocultural conditions** will first be related to the growing up of young people and their living environments, before the change in the education system and the role of sports in educational landscapes are outlined.

2.3.1   Growing Up of Children and Adolescents

Against the backdrop of social change, the growing up of children and adolescents in Germany has fundamentally changed in the past two to three decades. While children, at least in West Germany, grew up mainly in the family and—after half-day school—in the social neighborhood well into the second half of the 20th century, they now spend much more time in **educational institutions** and with educational professionals. From the daycare center to the all-day school to the organized leisure activities of extracurricular providers, the time of children and adolescents is increasingly pre-structured: "The pedagogical planning, design and staging […] of the living environment of the young generation are among the self-evident aspects of growing up at the beginning of the 21st century" (BMFSFJ 2013, p. 37). The 14th Children and Youth Report of the Federal Government accordingly states a significant **increase in public responsibility for the growing up** of children and adolescents (cf. Rauschenbach 2015). The question arises as to whether this can be understood as an opportunity or a risk.

In fact, children and adolescents in Germany have never had it as good as they do today. However, not all young people benefit from this to the same extent: "While some of the adolescents can look forward to a reasonably carefree future, secured by their parents with a net and double bottom, almost one in three young people in this country comes from a parental home that is either threatened by poverty, in which the parents do not work or do not have sufficient school qualifications" (BMFSFJ 2013, p. 54). There is much to suggest that the **social gap** between the winners and losers of growing up is widening. This is not only evident in findings on educational careers, but is also evidenced by massive inequalities in the areas of **development and health** of girls and boys (cf. Schmidt 2015). A comprehensive picture of the growing up of children and adolescents can therefore only be drawn against the background of different starting situations, which take into account both opportunities and risks.

Nevertheless, a look at the perspectives of young people shows that they are essentially satisfied with themselves and their environment. In relation to **childhood**, the Ferrero Children's Study states: "Most children feel very secure in their family and circle of friends" (Ferrero Deutschland 2013). The second World Vision Children's Study also confirms this assessment. The vast majority of children are "satisfied with their living conditions in family, leisure, circle of friends and school and feel comfortable. Their attitude towards what life has in store for them is expectant and therefore positive" (Hurrelmann and Andresen 2010, p. 16). The findings on **adolescence** come to similar results. Thus, the 16th Shell Youth Study states: "Today's young generation has not let its optimistic basic attitude be deterred by either the overall economic development ('economic and financial crisis') or the uncertain career paths and prospects" (Albert et al. 2010, p. 15; Shell Deutschland 2019). While the young people do see global problems, such as wars, energy crises or environmental destruction, they focus on their personal future.

In this sense, a pragmatic approach to the challenges of everyday life is typical for young people today. Since 2003, the Shell Study has used the term pragmatic generation and found that a **generation of ego-tacticians** has developed: "Ego -tacticians constantly sensitively ask the social environment for information about where they stand in their personal development" (Hurrelmann et al. 2003, p. 33). This does not mean that young people are fundamentally selfish, but rather that they flexibly take advantage of the opportunities that present themselves against the backdrop of dynamic living environments. Similarly, the NRW Youth Studies see a generation of **pragmatic order -seekers,** who are adept at "discovering orders and possibilities of order that work reasonably well and help them grow up" (Zinnecker et al. 2002, p. 18). Ultimately, this appears functional against the backdrop of changing living environments, particularly increasing educational pressure and increasingly confusing options for action: *You have many opportunities, choose the right ones!*

In contrast to earlier youth generations, Wopp (2007, p. 105) has coined the term **"as-well-as-generation"** for this basic attitude. The Sinus Study also speaks of new value configurations in the course of the "pragmatic turn", "which are no longer committed to the logic of 'either-or', but to the claim of 'both-and'" (Calmbach et al. 2012, p. 40). On the one hand, young people in uncertain times refer to traditional values, such as security, duty, friendship and family. On the other hand, these conservative values are "reinterpreted or symbolically updated and flanked by hedonistic, self-related development values and an individualistic ethos of achievement" (Calmbach et al. 2012, p. 40). This results in a value mix that focuses on "the feasible" and the present. Nevertheless, young people still show **social commitment.** Conservative and socio-ecologically oriented young people are involved in clubs and organizations such as sports clubs, church youth, scouts, rescue services or fire brigade (Calmbach et al. 2012, p. 84). Postmodern oriented young people were long considered "egotactically" motivated: It helps others, but it also helps their own CV. However, since the end of the 2010s, a rediscovery of political engagement has been observed, not least in relation to climate issues (Shell Deutschland 2019).

Overall, this results in a broad spectrum of the current **children and youth generation,** which is difficult to systematically organize. One of the few current attempts at organization is provided by the Sinus Life World Study, which spans a framework from "conservative-civic" to "adaptive-pragmatic" to "expeditive" young people (Calmbach et al. 2020). Nevertheless, even this qualitative study can only partially succeed in drawing a comprehensive **picture of "the" youth.** Quantitative research strategies are coarser in comparison and essentially refer to average values (e.g. Shell Deutschland 2019). Different views of younger and older people, girls and boys, poor and rich, educationally close and educationally distant, Germans and non-Germans, city and country dwellers, sporty and non-sporty, etc. are only minimally captured by these studies depending on their respective orientation. The **Children and Youth Reports** of the federal and state governments provide a summary overview of the upbringing of young people at regular intervals.

▶ **Literature Tip** J. Bundesministerium für Familie, Senioren, Frauen und Jugend [BMFSFJ] (2020). *16. Kinder- und Jugendbericht – Förderung demokratischer Bildung im Kindes- und Jugendalter.* Berlin: BMFSFJ.
    Every four years, the Federal Youth Ministry commissions a "Report on the living situation of young people and the services of child and youth welfare in Germany", which paints a picture of the upbringing of young people and sets a current focus each time.

2.3.2 Living Environments of Children and Adolescents

The living environments of children and adolescents are not unaffected by the sociocultural and socioeconomic conditions of the society in which they live. To characterize these specific conditions, the term **social setting** was long used, which can be described by factors such as location, time, activity, participating persons, and role (Bronfenbrenner 1981, pp. 95–115). The concept of living environment, on the other hand, is less static and includes the subjective perspectives of the involved actors.

▶ **Living Environment** The concept of living environment encompasses the diverse, individual and social, natural and cultural conditions in which human life is embedded. A person's living environment is "that everyday reality in which he exists through his physicality, in which he acts by shaping it and arranging it according to his life and experience needs, and by which he is treated, i.e., influenced and shaped" (Größing 1993, p. 100).

The living environments of children and adolescents are extremely diverse. Thus, media, cultural, and sports environments have a central importance for many young people (Grgic and Züchner 2013). The importance of sports for the growing up of young people is discussed in detail elsewhere (see Neuber 2020). In terms of *general* prerequisites, other important living environments will be outlined here as examples. The most important living environment for the grwoing up of children and adolescents is still the **family.** Normally, children are born into a family and grow up with it. The four basic functions of a family—provision, relationship, education, and formation —arise in daily cohabitation (cf. Schneewind 2008). The family is thus the primary socialization instance in the lives of young people, which means that "families have a special social capital, the so-called strong ties, i.e., the strong, close, and emotionally controlled relationships between the members" (Schneekloth and Pupeter 2010, p. 61). Even though family structures are now undergoing change, the "two-child nuclear family" is still the most common constellation. The relationship of young people to their parents and grandparents is more positive than in previous generations. Parents are appreciated as contact persons and advisors for practical life questions (Maschke et al. 2013, p. 29), while at the same time, young people are increasingly able to manage without their parents in sociocultural areas of life, such as fashion, media, and culture, at an earlier age.

The **peer group** then takes the place of the parents, gaining increasing importance in the lives of young people as they age. The vast majority of children and adolescents feel well integrated into a circle of friends. Having a "best friend" is reported by the vast majority of adolescents aged 10 to 18 years, with no significant difference between girls and boys (Maschke et al. 2013, pp. 53–54). A somewhat looser bond than that of a circle of friends characterizes the so-called clique, in which adolescents are somewhat less involved than in friendships. With the clique, children and adolescents primarily associate friendship, fun, chilling, parties, sports, and shared school time (see Fig. 2.2). Fights, talking about religious things, gossiping about others, and skipping school are mostly rejected by cliques, but approval of risky behavior in the clique increases with age (Maschke et al. 2013, pp. 58–64). Communication via social networks is a matter of course for adolescents, but in their understanding, it does not replace "offline relationships".

Regardless of whether it's a scene, clique, or community—communication and organization of leisure activities are increasingly being coordinated digitally (cf. Grigic and Züchner 2013). **Virtual living environments** thus belong to the places of growing up just like the real social immediate environment. Nothing has "changed the worlds of young people in the last two decades […] as fundamentally and sustainably as the developments that have taken place in the field of electronic media and the associated communication possibilities" (BMFSFJ 2013, p. 55). The most important online services in 2021 were WhatsApp, Instagram, TikTok, and Snapchat (MPFS 2021, p. 38). The number of "friends", which is usually visible in a specific number in social networks, serves as a kind of status symbol for many adolescents (Grgic and Züchner 2013, p. 177). In addition to the possibility of contacting friends, adolescents appreciate online networks

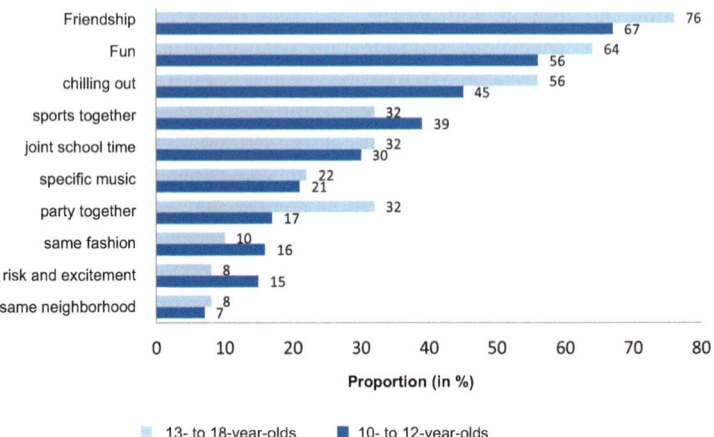

Fig. 2.2 What connects the clique/friend group among children (10–12 years) and adolescents (13–18 years)? (Mod. according to Maschke et al. 2013, pp. 55–56)

as a parent-free zone and as an opportunity to observe the network (Calmbach et al. 2012, pp. 52–53). Online networks are no longer understood by the majority of adolescents as a purely private space, but rather as a shapeable intermediate space, a kind of public privacy, where one lets others look into one's own life and can look into others' lives (Calmbach et al. 2012, p. 55).

The **school** also plays a central role as a living environment for children and adolescents. From the perspective of the adolescents, however, it is not only a place of learning, but above all a place of living. Clear temporal and organizational structures lead to it being "appreciated as a social contact and experience space" (Miethling 2000, p. 4). Adolescents therefore tend to enjoy going to school, which is particularly associated with the fact that they can meet friends here, exchange news, resolve conflicts, and make appointments (Calmbach et al. 2012, p. 60). The NRW Youth Study interprets this in the sense of a development of the school towards a "social event" (Maschke et al. 2013, p. 132). At the same time, however, young people also experience increased performance expectations at school with regard to their professional future. The increasing pressure to perform can also be identified by corresponding problems (Hurrelmann and Quenzel 2016). Girls apparently cope better with these expectations than boys. These are sometimes already considered as "educational losers", which not only brings individual, but also socio-political problems (Neuber 2020, pp. 71–91).

In addition to school and places of leisure, such as youth welfare institutions or sports clubs, **public spaces** are becoming increasingly important: "In the past, the private social space, the immediate environment of the parental home, the neighborhood, the street, played a central role in the successive exploration of the world, but also for some time parallel to school, nowadays [...] the spheres of the state, the market, and civil society are gaining increasing importance for the growing up" (BMFSFJ 2013, p. 55). Children and young people today naturally grow up in a world of goods and consumption, which on the one hand leads to further decision-making constraints, but on the other hand also to an increased importance of financial resources. Overall, the living environments of children and young people have become "more open, pluralistic, individual, provisional. Their integration into an ideologically and value-bound stable coordinate system becomes weaker, more fragile. Family-shaped patterns of life and milieus are often supplemented, broken through or fragmented by child and youth culturally staged forms of expression, styles, and preferences" (BMFSFJ 2013, p. 56). At the same time, childhood and youth are increasingly institutionalized and pedagogized.

2.3.3 Change of the Education System

After the so-called PISA shock at the beginning of the 2000s, the German education system was gripped by an eagerness for reform that had previously been considered almost impossible. From the daycare center to the school and into the university, state **educational institutions** were realigned. In addition, numerous non-state institutions, such as from child and youth welfare, musical-cultural education, or child and youth sports, were added. This revealed "the contours of a comprehensive and fundamental **structural change of the education system,** as it has developed in its present form in Germany since about the early 19th century" (Grunert and Wensierski 2008, p. 9). The change affects both the expansion of the public education mission from early childhood into adulthood (**"Lifelong Learning"**) and the increasing interlocking of previously separate educational institutions such as family, school, youth welfare, vocational training, and university (**"Educational Landscape"**). After two decades, however, the question arises as to how successful the reform efforts were. It is also worth looking at the different priorities set by the individual educational actors.

Thus, the **educational debate in schools** after the so-called PISA shock still revolves strongly around the question of the yield of the school system. Due to the restrictions of the COVID-19 pandemic, this view gained new significance at the beginning of the 2020s (Zierer 2021). To secure learning success, the school system was switched from input to **output control** as a result of the so-called Klieme expertise (Klieme et al. 2003). This was accompanied by increased standardization: "Educational standards are supposed to be the benchmark to capture this output; they thus become the decisive instrument of a control that starts from the output" (Kurz and Gogoll 2010, p. 230). School and teaching are understood in this view as an intentionally controllable event that leads to success through a targeted didactic-methodical staging. In this context, the **offer-and-use -model** became the decisive explanatory model for teaching effects (Helmke 2009). It is only logical that the school system regularly empirically records its own achievements through central learning status surveys and external school performance comparisons. This "empirical turn" is accompanied by numerous, often large-scale, impact studies (Terhart 2012).

With the **standardization** of school processes, there is a focus on a few competencies and (core) subjects that are supposed to be decisive for the future chances of students in the labor market. So-called minor subjects such as art, music, and physical education often fall out of sight. Not least the reactions to the Corona pandemic have shown that the school system is less oriented towards an all-round **personality development** than towards an efficiency-oriented alignment with job-related skills (Andresen et al. 2022). It is indeed questioned whether this one-sided orientation is actually beneficial for the later professional life of the adolescents (cf. Rauschenbach 2015). Nevertheless, the pressure on the school system to change, to open up to new tasks and target groups, to cooperate with new partners—and at the same time to meet the increased output expectations, is increasing. This pressure is passed on to the students, who try to meet the increasing **performance expectations** (cf. Hurrelmann and Quenzel, 2016).

In contrast, the **extracurricular education debate** distinguishes itself from the functional-pragmatic understanding of education in the school system. This would exclude central facets of education, such as physical-sensory, aesthetic, social, political, or reflective moments. In contrast, extracurricular actors establish a **comprehensive concept of education,** which understands education as active appropriation of the world, which occurs in different places, with different goals, and in different modalities (cf. Rauschenbach 2015). Education can therefore "only be adequately grasped if the diversity of educational locations and learning worlds, their interplay, their mutual interference and interdependence, but also their mutual isolation are perceived" (BMFSFJ 2005, p. 104). This means that educational success is no longer attributed solely to the school education system, but rather to a systematic **interlocking of different education providers** and offers. This gives extracurricular education actors more weight, but the perspective can also be understood as a relief for the school system—after all, the school is no longer solely responsible for the poor performance of students.

The basis of the extracurricular education discussion is a complex understanding of education (cf. Table 2.1), which distinguishes different types of learning ("learning or educational modalities") depending on the learning location, learning content, and staging of learning (Rauschenbach 2015):

- School learning primarily follows a **formal learning concept,** which is usually based on goal-oriented, structured, and mandatory education and instruction processes that are evaluated and certified.
- This is contrasted with an **informal learning concept** that happens more or less unplanned, unorganized, and voluntarily, e.g., in leisure time, but nevertheless provides important impulses for the development of adolescents.
- Offers of child and youth welfare are based on a **non-formal learning concept,** which is quite goal-oriented and planned, but in principle voluntary and not certified; this also applies to full-day offers in sports.

These analytically separated learning modalities are often difficult to distinguish in everyday life, which is why an integrative perspective has prevailed. Heim (2008) has proposed a model for sports, based on the 12th Children and Youth Report. He distinguishes between formal and non-formal **conditions,** e.g., in school and sports clubs. On the other hand, he differentiates between formal and informal **educational processes,** which occur under both formal and non-formal conditions (see Fig. 2.3). Thus, physical education in school can be understood as a formal educational process in a formal setting, while free movement play

Table 2.1 Learning modalities. (Neuber 2010, p. 13)

Informal Learning	Non-formal Learning	Formal Learning
Unplanned, unorganized, voluntary	Largely goal-oriented, organized, voluntary	Goal-oriented, structured, mandatory
Internal or external impulses	Courses, practice sessions, open offers	Education and instruction
Family, peer group, media	Youth center, sports club, adult education center	Kindergarten, school, university
No certificates	Mostly no certificates	Certificates

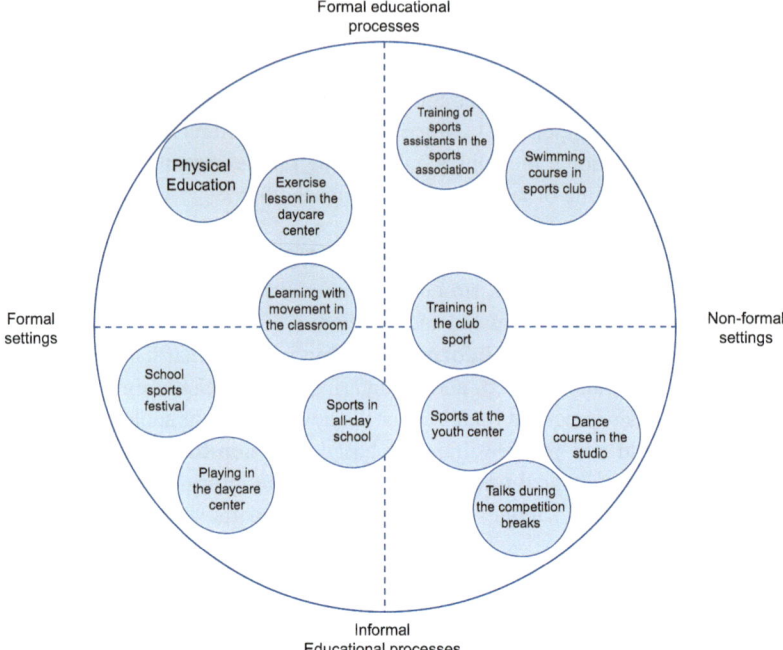

Fig. 2.3 Educational modalities in the context of movement, games, and sports. (Neuber and Golenia 2021, p. 60, mod. according to Heim 2008)

in a daycare center can be seen as an informal educational process under formal conditions. A group helper training in a sports association is a largely formalized educational process in a non-formal setting, while a conversation among young people during a competition break has an informal character and takes place under non-formal conditions (see Neuber and Golenia 2021). This model can be further expanded to include informal conditions (see Sect. 3.3.4).

2.3.4 Movement, Games, and Sports in Educational Landscapes

The expansion of the concept of education beyond school learning has led to a more comprehensive understanding of the educational process and the inclusion of all potential educational actors in the sense of an educational landscape. The idea of the **educational landscape** or educational network assumes that every person should be promoted according to their abilities and talents. Educational success should depend on individual potential and not on social origin (see Süßenbach 2021). Educational landscapes therefore start with the **educational biography** of each individual. Municipal education providers, such as daycare centers, schools, youth welfare institutions, churches, and sports clubs, cooperate to promote each child, each young person as optimally as possible. This requires a public **overall concept of education, formation, and care** in a municipality.

▶ **Educational Landscape ("Bildungslandschaft")** In summary, educational landscapes can be understood as "long-term, professionally designed networks on the subject of education, aimed at joint, planned action, desired by municipal politics, which, starting from the perspective of the learning subject, encompass formal places of education and informal learning worlds and refer to a defined local space" (Bleckmann and Durdel 2009, p. 12).

The **design of educational landscapes** varies considerably. For example, school-centered, cooperation-centered, or multidimensional educational landscapes are distinguished (see Eisnach 2011). However, the discourse on educational landscapes still revolves "very much around institutional planning and networking issues, the educational-theoretical foundations of cooperation often remain undefined" (Stolz 2009, p. 88). This also applies to the role of sports in educational networks. Initial approaches deal with determining the relationship between school and organized sports in all-day schooling (Pack and Ackermann 2011). Indeed, the **all-day school** offers numerous points of contact for municipal networking, e.g., in the joint planning of offers by schools and clubs. This also offers potential for quality development in an educational landscape (Bockhorst and Krumhöfner, 2020). In this respect, the all-day school can be seen as a **crystallization point for educational landscapes**, with extracurricular sports "usually institutionalized via the sports club and [...] thus becoming a cooperation partner for the school" (Süßenbach, 2021, p. 228). At the same time, new challenges arise for PE teachers with planning, organization, moderation, and consulting tasks (see Neuber and Jordens 2012).

All-day School in Municipal Educational Landscapes

The **transformation of the education system** is characterized by standardization and output orientation of the school, but also by a stronger networking of educational actors at the municipal level. The pivot of this educational cooperation is the **all-day school,** in which formal educational processes of the school are usually combined with non-formal educational offers of extracurricular actors (cf. Naul and Neuber 2021). The expansion of all-day schools was massively promoted from the very beginning. In the school year 2002/03, there were less than 5000 schools in all-day operation. In 2020, there were more than 21,000 schools (cf. KMK 2021). Few educational policy reform projects are likely to have changed the **school and educational landscape** so radically. Within just a decade, the all-day school has become an "integral part of the German education system" (Coelen and Stecher 2014, p. 5).

The introduction of the all-day school was associated with ambitious **objectives,** such as the individual promotion of all students, a changed learning culture, or equal opportunities in the education system (cf. Rauschenbach et al. 2012). The extent to which these ambitious goals have been achieved is controversial. Nevertheless, certain successes have been observed in targeted programs for reading and writing promotion or in the area of social skills (cf. StEG 2019). However, the balance is also somewhat sobering with regard to **all-day sports.** Targeted programs for motor talent promotion are as scarce as the promotion of social talents in sports. At least, the all-day operation should not have led to a decrease in the movement times of adolescents (cf. Naul and Neuber 2021). After a phase of expansion, the **development of all-day schools** stalled somewhat at the beginning of the 2020s. Over 60% of schools and more than 50% of students were in all-day operation in Germany at this time (cf. KMK 2021). With the nationwide legal entitlement to a full-day place in primary school from 2026, the reform zeal regarding the all-day school is likely to pick up speed again.

Movement, games, and sports activities are among the most popular and frequent offers of all-day schools. Every third all-day offer in Germany is a sports offer (Neuber et al. 2015). In this respect, all-day sports are not only a central offer for young people but also a great opportunity for school sports development (Neuber, 2020, pp. 137–158). However, it is necessary to think beyond physical education as an isolated subject and under-

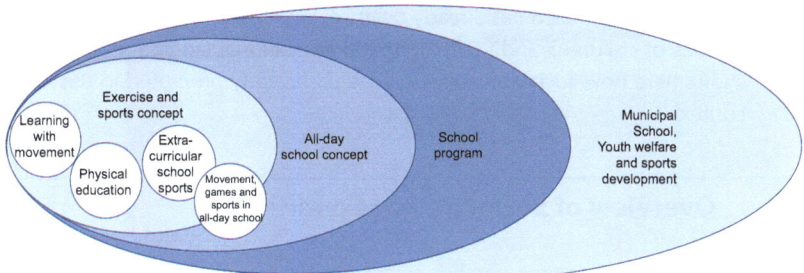

Fig. 2.4 Planning levels for movement, games, and sports in the all-day school. (Mod. according to Landessportbund NRW 2004, p. 11)

stand **school sports in the overall context** of an educational landscape (cf. Fig. 2.4). In this sense, four planning levels can be distinguished (Pack and Bockhorst 2011):

- At the level of the **school sports concept,** physical education, extracurricular school sports, and—closely linked to this—sports offers in all-day schools as well as learning with movement in other subjects are to be distinguished.
- The movement, play, and sports offers are embedded in the **all-day concept,** which, in addition to statements on the general promotion concept, includes information on homework supervision, lunch break, and leisure activities.
- Within the framework of the **school program,** the profile of the individual school is specified; with regard to movement, games, and sports, different approaches of the active and sports-oriented school are possible.
- At the level of **school, youth welfare, and sports development,** the guidelines of municipal education planning are drafted, into which the school sports development of the individual school is also integrated in the sense of the network idea.

▶ **Literature Tip** Süßenbach, J. (2021). I. Der Kinder- und Jugendsport in kommunalen Bildungslandschaften – wo geht die Reise hin? In N. Neuber (Ed.), Kinder- und Jugendsportforschung in Deutschland – Bilanz und Perspektive (pp. 225–243). Springer VS.

Jessica Süßenbach has already dealt several times with the opportunities of children's and youth sports in educational landscapes and shows here how social initiatives can be particularly promoted in this context.

2.4　Overview of Sociocultural Conditions

The sociocultural framework conditions are among the general basics of physical education. They form the **societal context,** in which movement, games and sports offers for children and adolescents take place (see Fig. 2.5). Starting from social transformation processes, modern societies have massively changed in the past two or three decades. They have become more individual and pluralistic and demand more responsibility from young people for their own growing up. These changes are also reflected in the behavior of children and adolescents, which is often described as "pragmatic". At the same time, the **living environments** of adolescents have changed and have become more digital, dynamic and public. The **education system** is also undergoing radical change. On the one hand, it is more output-oriented than before, especially in the so-called core subjects. On the

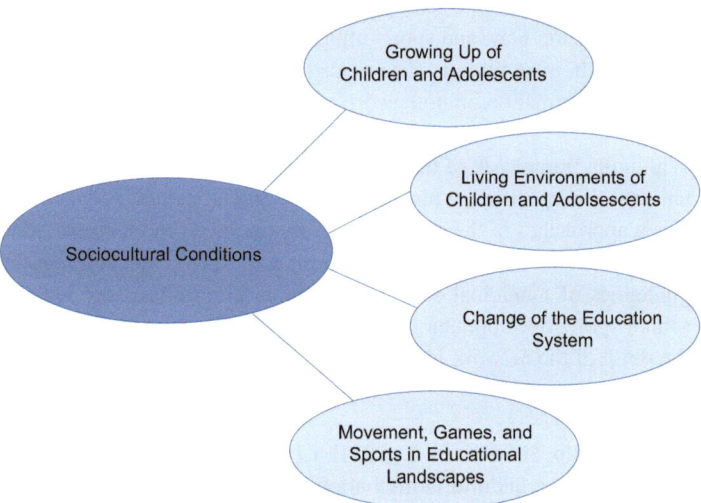

Fig. 2.5　Sociocultural framework conditions at a glance. (Own illustration)

other hand, education takes place at many locations and at many times. The idea of the municipal educational landscape illustrates this development. The extent to which sports play a central role in modern societies can be discussed. Nevertheless, **movement, games and sports offers** for children and adolescents take place under these conditions and must be staged against this background.

Reflection Questions

1. To what extent are movement, games and sports offers for children and adolescents dependent on the sociocultural framework conditions of a society?
2. Why is the responsibility for one's own biography in modern societies with the individual?
3. What is meant by the increase in public responsibility for the growing up of children and adolescents?
4. Why are the youth generations at the beginning of the 21st century referred to as "pragmatic" generations?
5. What distinguishes the different living environments of adolescents today?
6. What is meant by the fact that school is not only a place of learning, but also a place of life for many young people?
7. How do school and extracurricular education debates differ?
8. How does learning in school, all-day school and sports club differ?
9. Why does an educational landscape require a municipal overall concept of education, formation and care?
10. Why is the all-day school a crystallization point of sports in an educational landscape?

References

Albert, M., Hurrelmann, K., & Quenzel, G. (2010). Zusammenfassung. In Shell Deutschland (Eds.), *Jugend 2010. 16. Shell-Jugendstudie. Eine pragmatische Generation behauptet sich* (pp. 15–36). Frankfurt/M.: Fischer.

Andresen, S., Lips, A., Rusack, T., Schröer, W., Thomas, S., & Wilmes, J. (2022). *Verpasst? Verschoben? Verunsichert? Erste Ergebnisse der JuCo III-Studie – Erfahrungen junger Menschen während der Corona-Pandemie im Winter 2021.* Hildesheim: Universitätsverlag.

Beck, U. (1986). *Risikogesellschaft – Auf dem Weg in eine andere Moderne.* Frankfurt/M.: Suhrkamp.

Bleckmann, P., & Durdel, A. (2009). Einführung: Lokale Bildungslandschaften – die zwei-fache Öffnung. In P. Bleckmann & A. Durdel (Eds.), *Lokale Bildungslandschaften. Perspektiven für Ganztagsschulen und Kommunen* (pp. 11–17). Wiesbaden: VS.

Bockhorst, R., & Krumhöfner, A. (2020). Das Projekt „Qualität im Ganztag" – Förderung der Kooperationen zwischen Sportvereinen und Schulen im Landkreis Gütersloh. *Forum Kinder- und Jugendsport – Zeitschrift für Forschung, Transfer und Praxisdialog, 1*, 53–58. https://doi.org/10.1007/s43594-020-00012-7

BMFSFJ (Bundesministerium für Familie, Senioren, Frauen und Jugend). (2005). *12. Kinder- und Jugendbericht.* Berlin: BMFSFJ.

BMFSFJ (Bundesministerium für Familie, Senioren, Frauen und Jugend). (2013). *14. Kinder- und Jugendbericht – Bericht über die Lebenssituation junger Menschen und die Leistungen der Kinder- und Jugendhilfe in Deutschland.* Berlin: BMFSFJ.

BMFSFJ (Bundesministerium für Familie, Senioren, Frauen und Jugend). (2020). *16. Kinder- und Jugendbericht – Förderung demokratischer Bildung im Kindes- und Jugendalter.* Berlin: BMFSFJ.

Bronfenbrenner, U. (1981). *Die Ökologie der menschlichen Entwicklung – Natürliche und geplante Experimente.* Frankfurt/M.: Fischer.

Calmbach, M., Thomas, P. M., Borchard, I., & Flaig, B. (2012). *Wie Ticken Jugendliche? 2012. Lebenswelten von Jugendlichen im Alter von 14 bis 17 Jahren in Deutschland.* Düsseldorf: Altenberg.

Calmbach, M., Flaig, B., Edwards, J., Möller-Slawinski, H., Borchard, I., & Schleer, C. (2020). *SINUS-Jugendstudie 2020. Lebenswelten von Jugendlichen im Alter von 14–17 Jahren in Deutschland.* Bonn: Bundeszentrale für politische Bildung.

Coelen, T., & Stecher, L. (2014). *Einführung Ganztagsschule.* Weinheim, Basel: Beltz Juventa.

Eisnach, K. (2011). *Ganztagsschulentwicklung in einer kommunalen Bildungslandschaft. Möglichkeiten und Grenzen von Unterstützungsstrukturen.* Wiesbaden: VS.

Ferrero Deutschland (Eds.). (2013). *KinderStudie 2013. Die Welt mit Kinderaugen sehen. Ergebnisse einer Studie mit 4- bis 12-jährigen Kindern und deren Mütter.* Zugriff am 18.12.2014 http://www.emediarelease.de/uploads/downloads/3927_Zusammenfassung_kinderStudie_2013.pdf.

Grgic, M., & Züchner, I. (Eds.). (2013). *Medien, Kultur und Sport. Was Kinder und Jugendliche machen und ihnen wichtig ist. Die MediKuS-Studie.* Weinheim, Basel: Beltz Juventa.

Größing, S. (1993). *Bewegungskultur und Bewegungserziehung – Grundlagen einer sinnorientierten Bewegungspädagogik.* Schorndorf: Hofmann.

Größing, S. (2007). *Einführung in die Sportdidaktik* (9., überarbeitete und erweiterte edn.). Wiebelsheim: Limpert.

Grunert, C., & Wensierski, H. J. (2008). Jugend und Bildung – Modernisierungsprozesse und Strukturwandel von Erziehung und Bildung im 21. Jahrhundert – Einleitung. In C. Grunert & H. J. Wensierski (Eds.), *Jugend und Bildung – Modernisierungsprozesse und Strukturwandel von Erziehung und Bildung am Beginn des 21. Jahrhunderts* (pp. 9–15). Opladen: Barbara Budrich.

Güllich, A., & Krüger, M. (Eds.). (2022). *Sport. Ein Lehrbuch für das Sportstudium* (2. edn.). Berlin: Springer Spektrum.

Heim, C. (2008). Bewegung, Spiel und Sport im Kontext von Bildung. In W. Schmidt (Eds.), *Zweiter Deutscher Kinder- und Jugendsportbericht. Schwerpunkt: Kindheit* (pp. 21–42). Schorndorf: Hofmann.

Helmke, A. (2009). *Unterrichtsqualität und Lehrerprofessionalität. Diagnose, Evaluation und Verbesserung des Unterrichts* (2. edn.). Seelze-Velber: Kallmeyer.

Hornstein, W. (1997). Jugendforschung – Jugendpädagogik. In R. Fatke (Eds.), *Forschungs- und Handlungsfelder der Pädagogik* (Beiheft der Zeitschrift für Pädagogik, 36, pp. 13–50). Weinheim, Basel: Beltz.

Hurrelmann, K., Linssen, R., Albert, M., & Quellenberg, H. (2003). In Deutsche Shell (Eds.), *Jugend 2002 – Zwischen pragmatischem Idealismus und robustem Materialismus* (14. Shell-Jugendstudie, 4. edn., pp. 31–51). Frankfurt/M.: Fischer.

Hurrelmann, K., & Andresen, S. (Eds.). (2010). *Kinder in Deutschland 2010. 2. World Vision Kinderstudie.* Frankfurt am Main: Fischer.

Hurrelmann, K., & Quenzel, G. (2016). *Lebensphase Jugend – Eine Einführung in die sozialwissenschaftliche Jugendforschung* (13. überarbeitete Aufl.). Weinheim, Basel: Beltz Juventa.

Jank, W., & Meyer, H. (2020). *Didaktische Modelle.* Berlin: Cornelsen.

Klieme, E., Avenarius, H., Blum, W., Döbrich, P., Gruber, H., & Prenzel, M. (2003). *Zur Entwicklung nationaler Bildungsstandards. Eine Expertise.* Berlin: BMBF.

KMK (Kultusministerkonferenz). (2021). *Allgemeinbildende Schulen in Ganztagsform in den Ländern in der Bundesrepublik Deutschland – Statistik 2016 bis 2020.* Zugriff am 28.07.2022 https://www.kmk.org/fileadmin/Dateien/pdf/Statistik/Dokumentationen/GTS_2020_Bericht.pdf.

Kurz, D., & Gogoll, A. (2010). Standards und Kompetenzen. In N. Fessler, A. Hummel & G. Stibbe (Eds.), *Handbuch Schulsport* (pp. 227–244). Schorndorf: Hofmann.

Landessportbund NRW. (2004). *Sport im Ganztag. Schwerpunkte, Praxis, Perspektiven* (7. edn.). Duisburg: LSB.

Maschke, S., Stecher, L., Coelen, T., Ecarius, J., & Gusinde, F. (Eds.). (2013). *Appsolutely smart! Ergebnisse der Studie Jugend.Leben.* Bielefeld: WBV.

MPFS (Medienpädagogischer Forschungsverbund Südwest). (Eds.). (2021). *JIM-Studie 2021 – Jugend, Information, Medien.* Zugriff am 28.07.2022 unter https://www.mpfs.de/fileadmin/files/Studien/JIM/2021/JIM-Studie_2021_barrierefrei.pdf.

Miethling, W. D. (2000). Schülerinnen und Schüler im Unterrichtsalltag. *Sportpädagogik, 24*(6), 2–7.

Münchmeier, R. (1998). „Entstrukturierung" der Jugendphase – Zum Strukturwandel des Aufwachsens und zu den Konsequenzen für die Jugendforschung und Jugendtheorie. *Aus Politik und Zeitgeschichte, 31*, 3–13.

Mutz, M., & Burrmann, U. (2015). Integration. In W. Schmidt, N. Neuber, T. Rauschenbach, H. P. Brandl-Bredenbeck, J. Süßenbach & C. Breuer (Eds.), *Dritter Deutscher Kinder- und Jugendsportbericht. Kinder- und Jugendsport im Umbruch* (pp. 255–271). Schorndorf: Hofmann.

Naul, R., & Neuber, N. (2021). Sport im Ganztag – Zwischenbilanz und Perspektiven. In N. Neuber (Eds.), *Kinder- und Jugendsportforschung in Deutschland – Bilanz und Perspektive.* Wiesbaden: Springer.

Neuber, N. (2010). Informelles Lernen im Sport – ein vernachlässigtes Feld der allgemei-nen Bildungsdebatte. In N. Neuber (Eds.), *Informelles Lernen im Sport – Beiträge zur allgemeinen Bildungsdebatte* (pp. 9–31). Wiesbaden: VS.

Neuber, N. (2020). *Fachdidaktische Konzepte Sport – Zielgruppen und Voraussetzungen* (Basiswissen Lernen im Sport). Wiesbaden: Springer VS. https://doi.org/10.1007/978-3-658-28464-0.

Neuber, N. (Eds.). (2021a). Kinder- und Jugendsportforschung in Deutschland – Bilanz und Perspektive (Bildung und Sport, 26). Wiesbaden: Springer VS. https://doi.org/10.1007/978-3-658-30776-9.

Neuber, N. (2021b). *Fachdidaktische Konzepte Sport II – Themenfelder und Perspektiven* (Basiswissen Lernen im Sport). Wiesbaden: Springer VS. https://doi.org/10.1007/978-3-658-30249-8.

Neuber, N., & Golenia, M. (2021). Lernorte für Kinder und Jugendliche im Sport. In A. Güllich & M. Krüger (Eds.), *Sport in Kultur und Gesellschaft – Handbuch Sport und Sportwissenschaft* (pp. 55–71). Berlin, Heidelberg: Springer.

Neuber, N., & Jordens, J. (2012). Verschlafen die Sportlehrkräfte den Ganztag? – Zum Wandel der Sportlehrerrolle in kommunalen Bildungslandschaften. *Sportunterricht, 61*(10), 291–296.

Neuber, N., Kaufmann, N., & Salomon, S. (2015). Ganztag und Sport. In W. Schmidt, N. Neuber, T. Rauschenbach, H. P. Brandl-Bredenbeck, J. Süßenbach & C. Breuer (Eds.), *Dritter Deutscher Kinder- und Jugendsportbericht. Kinder- und Jugendsport im Umbruch* (pp. 416–443). Schorndorf: Hofmann.

Neuber, N., & Salomon, S. (2015). Aufwachsen im Wandel. In W. Schmidt, N. Neuber, T. Rauschenbach, H.-P. Brandl-Bredenbeck, J. Süßenbach & C. Breuer (Eds.), Dritter Deutscher Kinder- und Jugendsportbericht: Kinder- und Jugendsport im Umbruch (pp. 24–49). Schorndorf: Hofmann.

Pack, R.-P., & Ackermann, S. (2011). Sport als Netzwerkpartner in kommunalen Bildungslandschaften. In M. Krüger & N. Neuber (Eds.), *Bildung im Sport – Beiträge zu einer zeitgemäßen Bildungsdebatte* (pp. 233–249). Wiesbaden: VS.

Pack, R.-P., & Bockhorst, R. (2011). Bewegung, Spiel und Sport in Ganztagsschulen als Impulsgeber für die Entwicklung von kommunalen Bildungslandschaften. In R. Naul (Eds.), *Bewegung, Spiel und Sport in der Ganztagsschule – Bilanz und Perspektiven* (pp. 164–181). Aachen: Meyer & Meyer.

Rauschenbach, T., Arnoldt, B., Steiner, C., & Stolz, H.-J. (2012). *Ganztagsschule als Hoffnungsträger für die Zukunft? Ein Reformprojekt auf dem Prüfstand. Expertise des Deutschen Jugendinstituts (DJI) im Auftrag der Bertelsmann Stiftung.* Gütersloh: Bertelsmann Stiftung.

Rauschenbach, T. (2015). Umbrüche im Bildungswesen. In W. Schmidt, N. Neuber, T. Rauschenbach, H. P. Brandl-Bredenbeck, J. Süßenbach & C. Breuer (Eds.), *Dritter Kinder- und Jugendsportbericht. Kinder- und Jugendsport im Umbruch* (pp. 50–77). Schorndorf: Hofmann.

Reinders, H. (2006). *Jugendtypen zwischen Bildung und Freizeit – Theoretische Präzisierung und empirische Prüfung einer differenziellen Theorie der Adoleszenz.* Münster: Waxmann.

Rosa, H. (2005). *Beschleunigung – Die Veränderung der Zeitstrukturen in der Moderne.* Frankfurt/M.: Suhrkamp.

Schmidt, W. (2015). Informeller Sport. In W. Schmidt, N. Neuber, T. Rauschenbach, H. P. Brandl-Bredenbeck, J. Süßenbach & C. Breuer (Eds.), *Dritter Deutscher Kinder- und Jugendsportbericht. Kinder- und Jugendsport im Umbruch* (pp. 201–216). Schorndorf: Hofmann.

Schmidt, W., Neuber, N., Rauschenbach, T., Brandl-Bredenbeck, H. P., Süßenbach, J., & Breuer, C. (Eds.). (2015). *Dritter Deutscher Kinder- und Jugendsportbericht. Kinder- und Jugendsport im Umbruch*. Schorndorf: Hofmann.

Schneekloth, U., & Pupeter, M. (2010). Familie als Zentrum: Bunt und vielfältig, aber nicht für alle Kinder gleich verlässlich. In K. Hurrelmann & S. Andresen (Eds.), *Kinder in Deutschland 2010. 2. World Vision Kinderstudie* (pp. 61–94). Frankfurt am Main: Fischer.

Schneewind, K. A. (2008). Sozialisation in der Familie. In K. Hurrelmann, M. Grundmann & S. Walper (Eds.), *Handbuch Sozialisationsforschung* (7., vollständig überarbeitete edn., pp. 256–273). Weinheim, Basel: Beltz.

Schubert, K., & Klein, M. (2022). *Das Politiklexikon* (7., aktualisierte und erweiterte Aufl.). Bonn: Bundeszentrale für politische Bildung.

Shell Deutschland (Eds.). (2019). *Jugend 2019 – Eine Generation meldet sich zu Wort* (18. Shell-Jugendstudie). Weinheim, Basel: Beltz.

Stolz, H. J. (2009). Schule und Jugendhilfe als Partner. *Deutsche Zeitschrift für Kommunalwissenschaften, 48*(1), 77–90.

StEG (Studie zur Entwicklung von Ganztagsschulen). (2019). Individuelle Förderung – Potenziale der Ganztagsschule. Frankfurt am Main: StEG-Konsortium.

Süßenbach, J. (2021). Der Kinder- und Jugendsport in kommunalen Bildungslandschaften – wo geht die Reise hin? In N. Neuber (Eds.), *Kinder- und Jugendsportforschung in Deutschland – Bilanz und Perspektive* (pp. 225–243). Springer VS. https://doi.org/10.1007/978-3-658-30776-9_11.

Terhart, E. (2012). Wie wirkt Lehrerbildung? Forschungsprobleme und Gestaltungsfragen. *Zeitschrift für Bildungsforschung, 2*(1), 3–21.

Tillmann, K.-J. (2010). *Sozialisationstheorien. Eine Einführung in den Zusammenhang von Gesellschaft, Institution und Subjektwerdung* (2., erweiterte Aufl.). Reinbek: Rowohlt.

Vorländer, H. (2013). Krise, Kritik und Szenarien: Zur Lage der Demokratie. *Zeitschrift für Politikwissenschaft, 23*(2), 267–277.

Wopp, C. (2007). Lebenswelt, Jugendkulturen und Sport in der Schule. In R. Laging (Eds.), *Neues Taschenbuch des Sportunterrichts. Kompaktausgabe* (pp. 104–122). Baltmannsweiler: Schneider.

Zierer, K. (2021). *Ein Jahr zum Vergessen – Wie wir die Bildungskatastrophe nach Corona verhindern*. Freiburg: Herder.

Zinnecker, J., Behnken, I., Maschke, S., & Stecher, L. (2002). *Null zoff & voll busy – Die erste Jugendgeneration des neuen Jahrhunderts*. Opladen: Leske + Budrich.

Pedagogical Basics

3

Abstract

This chapter deals with the central pedagogical prerequisites of movement, games, and sports offerings for children and adolescents. Starting from the concept of pedagogical action, the sport as a pedagogical field of action, sports pedagogical justifications, sports pedagogical action in the sense of an education to and through sport, as well as learning locations for children and adolescents in sport are presented. An excursion to educational PE complements the chapter.

3.1   Introduction

An educational interpretation of sports particularly aims at promoting children and adolescents. For this, **sports pedagogy** provides relevant justification patterns. It can be understood as that sub-discipline of educational and sports science that "examines the sporting and playful physical activity in its institutionalized and non-institutionalized forms primarily under the motives of education, formation, socialization and learning" (Meinberg 1996, p. 17). Sports pedagogy mainly deals with **questions of meaning and justification** of educational action in sports and thus forms an educational framework. Sports didactics, on the other hand, deals with "concrete situations, phenomena and processes of teaching and learning" in sports (Scheid and Oesterhelt 2022, p. 29). In this respect, sports pedagogy rather asks for justifications and goals of sports-related promotion, i.e., the "why?" and "what for?", while **sports didactics** asks for the "what?" and the "how?", i.e., the contents and methods (cf. Prohl and Scheid 2022).

N. Neuber, *Didactics of Physical Education and Sport*,
https://doi.org/10.1007/978-3-658-47188-0_3

Similar to sports didactics, sports pedagogy focuses largely on **school and school sports**. This is institutionally conditioned because sports science institutes mainly qualify PE teachers. On the other hand, it is related to the fact that the aesthetic subjects of art, music, and physical education are particularly challenged to deal with "the question of the meaning of their teaching content and thus also the justification of their existence as a school subject" (Prohl and Scheid 2022, p. 10). In addition to school sports, there are a number of extracurricular fields of action in which young people move and play sports. **Children's and youth sports** include, for example, club sports, sports in youth welfare, informal sports, and commercial sports (cf. Schmidt et al. 2015). The justifications and objectives for these fields are quite different. Sometimes they do not even explicitly pursue educational goals. Nevertheless, they can be educationally effective. For understanding **sports pedagogical action**, it is helpful to recall the pedagogical foundations of sports and physical education.

3.2 Basic Concepts

The starting point of the chapter is the concept of **educational action,** which is understood as a mediation relationship between teachers and learners and is fundamentally ambivalent and asymmetrically designed (Helsper 2010). **Sports pedagogical action** can accordingly be understood as an "interactive-asymmetric mediation relationship" in the field of movement, games, and sports. At the core of this mediation relationship lies the **educational relationship** between educators and those to be educated—or "educator" and "pupil" –, which is characterized by a positive emotional bond, but also by a competence and power gradient that cannot be resolved in principle (Trenz 2019). **Basic forms of educational action** are considered to be education ("Erziehung") and formation ("Bildung"). In addition, teaching, organization, diagnosis, counseling, help, and care are central forms of pedagogical activity (Neuber 2007, pp. 73–81).

▶ **Educational Physical Education ("Erziehender Sportunterricht")** For sports pedagogical action, the concept of educational PE is crucial, which is characterized by the dual mandate of an *education for* and *through sports* and is structured by corresponding pedagogical principles and perspectives (cf. Prohl 2022).

The **sports pedagogical field of action** is characterized by specific, non-exchangeable learning opportunities, for example, by a high degree of identification and openness, authenticity, and interaction. At the same time, it is an ambivalent field of experience, in which success and confirmation can be experienced on the one hand, but failure and exclusion on the other (cf. Grimminger 2015). **Sports pedagogical justifications** draw on different scientific disciplines, e.g., anthropology, developmental and learning theory, health science, or school culture research. They help to derive and normatively justify sports pedagogical objectives (cf. Balz et al. 2022). In addition to school, further **learning locations** for children and adolescents in sports can be described, including sports clubs, all-day schools, informal and commercial sports offers. Against the backdrop of a complex understanding of education, these learning locations offer different learning potentials (Neuber and Golenia 2021).

3.3 Foundations

Educational action is a phenomenon of modern times. Only when the dominance of the church was overcome with the beginning of the Enlightenment, when feudal class orders dissolved and industrialization demanded trained workers, was differentiated educational action necessary (cf. Oelkers 2001). Initial designs of educational action understood the **educator as a craftsman,** who only had to perform the correct actions in the sense of a "pedagogical machine" to achieve the desired effects. A similar logic also follows the idea of the **educator as a gardener,** who only has to ensure the "natural" growth of the child so that it develops appropriately. This "pedagogy of letting grow" is still leading for large parts of reform pedagogy today (Idel and Ulrich 2017). A critique of these naive understandings refers to the so-called **structural technology deficit** of educational action (Luhmann and Schorr 1982). Educational success cannot be linearly pursued, let alone methodically controlled. Rather, educational action is fundamentally uncertain and ambivalent: "The educator must act with intentions of change without being able to have cause-effect relationships, and must expect unintended side effects that can thwart his intention" (Helsper 2010, pp. 18–19).

In addition, educational action takes place in an interactive **mediation relationship** between "educator" and "pupil", which is accompanied by differences in knowledge, competence and power. The pedagogy in the humanities understood this relationship as "the passionate relationship of a mature person to a becoming person, for his own sake, that he may come to his life and his form" (Nohl 1963, p. 134). This **educational reference** further developed into the teacher-student interaction, which emphasizes the reciprocity of the relationship between teachers and learners (cf. Trenz 2019). The central starting point remains the establishment of a **positive relationship,** which the psychologist Carl Rogers

(1989) describes with the basic attitudes "acceptance", "empathy" and "authenticity". Against this backdrop, the authoritarian, democratic and laissez-faire style were derived as three central **educational styles** that characterize the relationship between teachers and learners (Tausch and Tausch, 1998). However, the relationship between educators and those to be educated remains fundamentally tense; the principal asymmetry is insurmountable.

Likewise, the relationship between **individual case and rule knowledge** is fundamentally not resolvable. Educational action usually targets a larger group of people, which means that educators are dependent on referring to generally valid, more or less scientifically secured rules for the design of their actions. Without this **"subsumption logic"** they would be lost in everyday pedagogical life. On the other hand, the specificity of the individual case "cannot be subjected to any abstract rule or technologizable procedure, but always requires a case-reconstructive component, in which generalized explanation patterns and theoretical knowledge stocks must be checked, revised and interpreted for their case appropriateness" (Helsper 1996, p. 532). Therefore, pedagogical activity is fundamentally in a field of tension between abstract rule knowledge and concrete case reference.

▶ **Educational action** can thus be summarized as "an interactive-asymmetrical mediation relationship in the tension between understanding the case and rule knowledge" (Helsper 2010, p. 31), which takes place under fundamentally uncertain, ultimately always ambivalent conditions of action.

The **ambivalences** are highly dependent on sociocultural conditions. Against the backdrop of societal upheavals of modernity (see Chap. 2), it can therefore be assumed that "the antinomic basic tensions of teacher action […] experience an increase and generate new demands for reflection and action for teachers" (Helsper 1996, p. 521). In this sense, Helsper (2010) defines four **antinomies of pedagogical action** in modernity: proximity vs. distance, autonomy vs. compulsion, interaction vs. organization, and cultural difference vs. unity (Neuber 2007, pp. 64–73). Thus, pedagogical action, for example, aims at the autonomy of learners, but at the same time takes place against the backdrop of social norms and institutional rules that must not be circumvented. In this situation, teachers can only act in an **"as-if mode"**: "They presuppose the autonomy of possible assumption of responsibility and thus the possible autonomy of the child", although this is not actually given (Helsper 2010, p. 20).

In this paradoxical situation, teachers can resort to various **basic forms of pedagogical action**. Education and formation are seen as central forms of pedagogical action. Other basic forms are teaching, organization, diagnosis, counseling, and help (Krüger and Helsper 2010). With regard to the increased pedagogical challenges in all-day schooling, care can also be added as another form. This results in a **spectrum of pedagogical forms of action,** ranging from activities with a comparatively pronounced dominance of the teacher—such as educating, diagnosing, and helping—through more or less balanced activities— such as teaching and organizing—to activities—such as forming, caring for, and advising—where the leadership function of the teacher recedes into the background (see Fig. 3.1). Ultimately, this shows a tendency that does not question the responsibility of teachers, but at the same time aims at increasing **self-determination** of young people in modern societies (Neuber 2007, pp. 73–81). Against the backdrop of these general considerations on pedagogical action, the following presents *specific* prerequisites, justifications, forms of action, and learning locations of *sports*pedagogical action.

▶   **Literature tip** Krüger, H.-H. & Helsper, W. (Eds.). (2010). *Einführung in die Grundbegriffe und Grundfragen der Erziehungswissenschaft* (9th ed.). Wiesbaden: Springer VS.

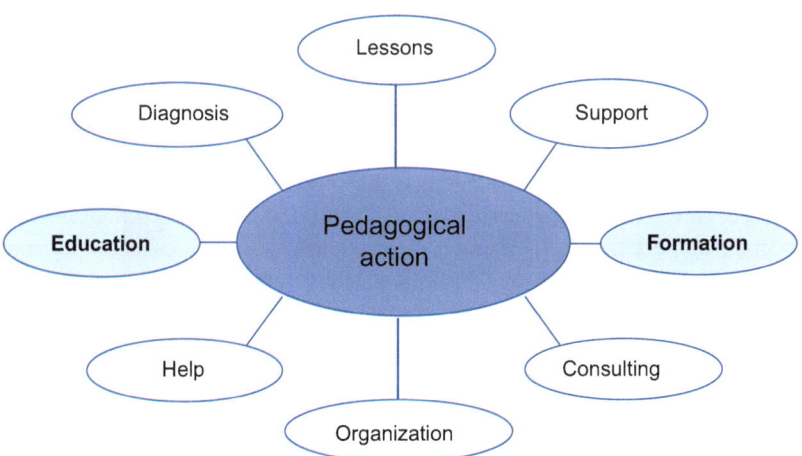

Fig. 3.1 Basic forms of pedagogical action in modernity. (Mod. according to Neuber 2007, p. 81)

In their classic work, Heinz-Hermann Krüger and Werner Helsper provide an overview of basic pedagogical terms such as education, training, teaching, socialization, and learning.

3.3.1 Sport as a Field of Pedagogical Action

Movement, games, and sports can be staged with pedagogical intent, but they do not per se have pedagogical significance. In the sense of **sports pedagogical action,** playful and sporty movements must be checked for their pedagogical potential and designed accordingly. Sport is a historically grown, time-dependent part of culture, determined by the prevailing values and norms of a society. The dominant movement patterns are an expression of the values that are significant in a culture. Sport can thus be understood as a **mirror of society** (see Beckers 1993, pp. 13–14). In this sense, sport in modern Western societies is characterized by a pronounced **performance orientation**—regardless of whether it is competitive, health, or trend sports (Neuber 2021b, pp. 95–114). Basic principles of capitalist societies—such as objectification, economization, or maximization—are highly reflected in this "sporty sport" (Heinemann 1989). At the same time, this understanding also affects the "non-sporty sport", e.g., into pedagogical learning places like school.

Against this background, sport is a **ambivalent field of experience,** in which individual athletic achievements can be recognized, leading to success and affirmation on one hand. On the other hand, experiences of failure and exclusion can also lead to significant disregard (see Grimminger 2015). These negative experiences are all the more formative as they are directly experienced "on one's own body". In this respect, the technology deficit, which is characteristic of pedagogical action, can also be transferred to sports and thus in a special way to **sports pedagogical action**: Sports pedagogical stagings *can,* but they *do not have to* succeed. Nevertheless, the physical embodiment of movement experiences offers specific, non-exchangeable learning opportunities that distinguish sports from other fields and make it interesting for educational processes (Neuber and Gebken, 2009). These include the following aspects:

- Sports is one of the most common and important activities in the lives of children and adolescents. Physical education is the most popular subject in school; with binding rates of up to 80%, sports clubs reach more young people than any other youth organization, and about 90% of all adolescents engage in self-organized physical activity (Breuer et al. 2020). Therefore, participation in sports can be confidently referred to as a "youth-specific age norm" (Zin-necker 1991). Above all, this great popularity leads to a high degree of **identi-fication,** which can be seen as a favorable prerequisite for learning processes.

- The **voluntariness** and fundamental **openness** of sports not only facilitate access to athletic activities, but also offer good opportunities for variable task settings. Within the framework of physical education, different abilities and interests of young people can be well addressed through methodological differentiations (cf. Pfitzner and Neuber 2012). The supposed incompatibility of equality and difference, which ostensibly opposes a common teaching of sports-motivated and sports-unmotivated individuals, can thus be overcome in the sense of a "pedagogy of participation" (Tiemann 2015).
- The **feedback** central to learning processes in sports usually occurs directly, as children and adolescents experience the effectiveness of their own actions directly "on their own bodies". The elementary importance of self-efficacy experiences is particularly well documented in the area of early childhood movement education. Self-efficacy beliefs have a strong motivating effect: situations that appear controllable are revisited, and one's own competence expectation boosts one's own self-esteem (see Zimmer 2019). Immediate feedback is highly significant for all forms of learning.
- The difficulty of pretending during movement activities and the immediacy of physical experience ensure a high degree of **authenticity** in learning processes. One's own abilities and the abilities of others are obvious in most movement situations—as are one's own and others' inabilities. This plays a major role especially in pedagogically uninfluenced (sports) youth scenes (see Bindel 2017). At the same time, physical activities are always associated with emotional processes. Thus, participation in sports proves to be a comparatively basic, "real" activity in which young people can directly experience themselves and others, which in turn is considered a favorable prerequisite for learning processes.
- Most sports activities take place in **interaction** with other people, offering special opportunities for cooperation and competition experiences based on physical confrontations. By participating in sports together, young people enter into a "movement relationship that varies from case to case and task to task" (Funke-Wieneke 1997, p. 34). At the same time, sports activities in childhood and adolescence are among the most common reasons for meeting up; the sports club is considered a "hub" of social networks in adolescence. Intensive peer contacts are among the central prerequisites for learning processes in adolescence.

- Through the presentation of one's own body, the field of movement, games, and sports opens up opportunities for **aesthetic experiences,** which can also lie beyond linguistic-discursive confrontation. Fritsch (2007) understands aesthetic behavior, starting from the sensory-driven processes of perception ("Aisthesis") and design ("Poiesis"), as an independent way of processing world experience. Young people can express what they have experienced, what is important to them, through movement. In contrast to discursive, conceptual confrontation, aesthetic-symbolic action offers the possibility to articulate the "unspeakable". Especially informal music and dance scenes offer special potentials for this.

3.3.2 Sports Pedagogical Justifications

The specific learning opportunities of movement, games, and sports are not only interesting for adolescents, but they are also particularly suitable for a pedagogical approach. However, this should not be done randomly, but should be justified and consciously staged. Critics warn against an **instrumentalization of sports** and advocate for putting the "sport in itself" in the foreground. However, such an unaffected sport does not exist, as sport—like any other societal field—is always an expression of culture-dependent values and norms (cf. Beckers 1993). In fact, physical activities of children and adolescents are rarely free from pedagogical instrumentalization, as the corresponding debate in the first half of the 1990s shows (cf. Scherler 1997). Therefore, the **justification and reflection** of pedagogical objectives and methods appear all the more important. Sport can be driven by various motives and can be staged from different perspectives (cf. Laging 2017; Balz et al. 2022; Scheid and Prohl 2022). Accordingly, different justification patterns can be used for the **pedagogical staging** of movement, games, and sports (cf. Fig. 3.2):

- **Anthropological justifications** of movement, games, and sports refer to the "nature" or "essence" of humans or to a corresponding image of humans. In line with the ideas of the Enlightenment, the image of humans as active, acting, and decision-making social beings has prevailed in pedagogical anthropology. Essential characteristics are maturity and autonomy (Meinberg 1984, pp. 60–61). At the same time, humans are seen not only as intellectual but also as physical beings who move and must move because it is part of being human. From this, specific reference fields for an anthropological justification of sports activities can be derived with the body/physical theme, the movement theme, the play theme, and the performance theme (cf. Grupe 1985).

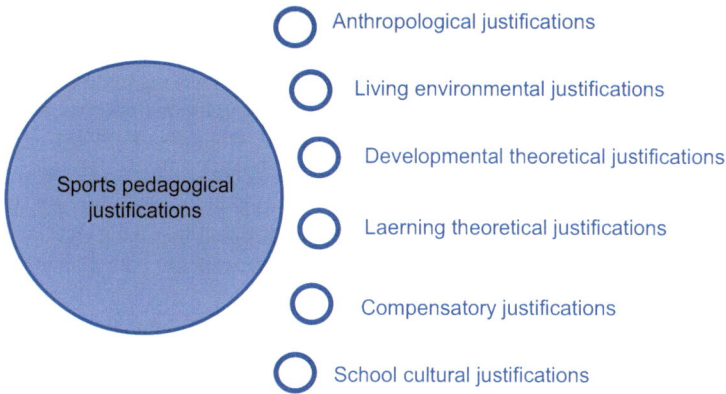

Fig. 3.2 Sports pedagogical justifications. (Own illustration)

- **Living environmental justifications** of movement, games, and sports take up the everyday reality of children and adolescents in both a subjective and objective sense (see Sect. 2.3.2). In the first case, the experiences of young people are focused on, in the second case, the focus is on their living conditions and experiences, especially on people and places that are accessible to them (Hildebrandt 1993, pp. 259–260). Conditions of experience related to movement are ambivalent: on the one hand, they promise joyful experiences to adolescents, on the other hand, they are impaired in many ways, for example by spatial and temporal limitations. In childhood research, cultural-optimistic views are distinguished from cultural-pessimistic views in this context (Neuber 2020, pp. 31–50).
- **Developmental theoretical justifications** of movement, games, and sports assume a complex relationship between movement and development. As an ordered sequence of related changes that remain constant across different situations, development is a central motive of sports pedagogical justifications (cf. Neuber and Scheid 2021). Thus, movement experiences influence intelligence development in preschool age. In the phase of "sensorimotor intelligence", cognitive structures in the brain even develop almost exclusively through movement actions (cf. Zimmer 2020). Even in later stages of development, the "grasping" of the environment plays a central role in promoting development, e.g., for the development of self-concept, social behavior, or creativity (cf. Neuber 2007, pp. 22–27).
- **Learning theoretical justifications** for movement, games, and sports pick up on developmental theoretical considerations and continue them in relation to

targeted cognitive learning processes. The starting point is the concept of the Active School, which uses movement activities not only in physical education, but in all areas of the school (cf. Laging 2017). The focus of the learning theory justifications lies in the promotion of the so-called executive functions Inhibition, Updating (working memory), and cognitive flexibility (Boriss 2015) (cf. Sect. 7.3.2). Cognitive psychological studies prove that these basic cognitive abilities play a central role in self-regulation and thus for school learning in general. At the same time, it is undisputed that the executive functions can be well promoted through targeted movement tasks (Pfitzner et al. 2021).

- **Compensatory justifications** for movement, games, and sports are closely linked to everyday life and developmental theoretical justification patterns. Not least after the COVID-19 pandemic, motor and health impairments in children and adolescents were identified (cf. Schmidt et al. 2021). In addition, there is increased developmental pressure in school, which can lead to a lack of coping with age-specific developmental tasks (cf. Hurrelmann and Quenzel 2016). Movement, games, and sports are attributed a high potential to prevent health impairments. Thus, Brodtmann (2008) distinguishes between proportional and behavioral preventive aspects of health promotion in school sports. This compensatory justification for movement activities in school is also taken up in the context of school development.

- **School cultural justifications** for movement, games, and sports aim at the special importance of movement activities for school culture. The school should not only be understood as a learning space, but also as a living space in which children and adolescents feel comfortable, in which they can develop and which they can help shape (Laging 2017). In this sense, movement, games, and sports offers can contribute to a stronger rhythmization of the school day, to more action-oriented teaching methods in all subjects, and to an active school life. Here too, concepts for the Active School can be used as a basis for justification (Neuber 2020, pp. 137–158). At the same time, compensatory arguments in times of long (all-day) school days form a central line of justification.

▶ **Literature tip** Balz, E., Reuker, S., Scheid, V. & Sygusch, R. (Eds.). (2022). *Sportpädagogik - Eine Grundlegung.* Stuttgart: Kohlhammer.

With their anthology, the authors undertake a self-assurance of sports pedagogy by presenting sports pedagogical starting points, basics, orientations, and research.

3.3.3 Sports Pedagogical Action

In reference to the general definition of pedagogical action, *sports* pedagogical action can be understood as an interactive-asymmetrical mediation relationship in the field of movement, games, and sports. The antinomic conditions of action of modernity can also be related to sports. *Specific* antinomies are particularly described with the concept of the **double paradox of physical education** (cf. Prohl 2010, p. 100). In addition to the basic contradiction between qualification and selection, there is the contradiction between "sports as subjective fulfillment of meaning", as many children and adolescents appreciate outside of school, and sports as a "compulsory school event", which is subject to school curricula and obligations (cf. Fig. 4.1 and 5.1). Finally, the basic forms of pedagogical action can also be transferred to the field of sports pedagogy. As central tasks of **pedagogical action in sports**, education and training have already been highlighted (see Chap. 1). They refer to the double objective of an "education to sports" and an "education through sports", which is guiding for large parts of school, but also extracurricular sports (cf. Scherler 1997).

▶ **Education for sport** aims at structuring the thinking, feeling, and actions of children and adolescents in the field of sports, i.e., it is about the transmission of skills and abilities, knowledge and attitudes, which are necessary for participating in sports in modern societies (cf. Beckers 2009).

In reference to Brezinka (1990), education can also be understood as a process of targeted influence towards behavior considered valuable. In this context, it is necessary to clarify what is considered "valuable". This question refers to the **educational objectives,** which are highly influenced by society and culture and must be normatively justified. Against the backdrop of social change, educational objectives are increasingly under pressure to justify their legitimacy. Sometimes even the "end of education" is prophesied, "because educators have lost their goal and normative ideas, especially the possibilities of a binding canon of norms for the future" (Heitger 1999, p. 140). In addition, the question of **educational means** needs to be clarified. If education strives to make itself redundant, an education through "compulsion" or "guidance" appears at least obsolete. In sports pedagogy, Funke-Wieneke (1999) even speaks of "self-education", which, however, is hardly possible according to common understanding, as education requires at least one educator and one to be educated.

▶ **Education through sport** uses movement, games, and sports activities to achieve objectives that go beyond sports, such as promoting self-confidence or the social competence of adolescents. Such promotion is entirely intentional in the sense of a classical educational process. Often, however, education through sport is also understood as an educational process in the sense of formation ("Bildung").

In this case, the learning process eludes educational access because **educational processes** are reflexive in the sense of "self-formation", as "the actual act of education, the appropriation of the world [...] shifts into the subject itself" (Meinberg 1996, p. 56). Nevertheless, educational processes can be stimulated. Compared to education, formation is aimed at expanding individual perspectives and thus at the subject's ability to develop its own standpoint and to shape its life independently in social responsibility (Beckers 2009). In this **emancipatory sense,** education can be understood as "that constitution of man" which "enables him to bring both himself and his relations to the world 'in order'" (Litt 1963, p. 11). The dual task of education for and through sport is particularly reflected in the works on **educational physical education** (cf. Prohl 2022).

Educational Physical Education ("Erziehender Sportunterricht")
After a phase of pragmatism in the 1970s/80s, school sports experienced a pedagogical renaissance in the 1990s. Based on the considerations of the Education Commission NRW (1995), more weight was given to the idea of education, leading to the so-called **dual mandate** of education for and through sports (Beckers 2000). In the North Rhine-Westphalian curriculum, the dual mandate is: Access to movement, game and sports culture and promoting development through movement, game and sports (MSWWF NRW 1999). School sports should thus "impart both subject-specific skills, abilities and knowledge as well as initiate attitudes and stances necessary for a judgement and action-capable participation not only in sports, but in social and political design processes" (Beckers 2000, p. 86). Based on the dual mandate, the teaching is explicitly understood as **educational physical education**. As such, it follows **pedagogical principles** such as those

of multiperspectivity, experience and action orientation, reflection, under-standing and value orientation (MSWWF NRW 1999).

The subject of educational physical education is defined in the form of broad **content areas** that each include both forms of self-determined movement and forms of standardized competitive sports, e.g. "Running, Jumping, Throwing—Athletics" or "Moving in Water—Swimming". This expands the spectrum of standardized (performance) sports in the sense of the triad **movement, game and sports**. In addition, with "Perceiving the Body and Developing Movement Abilities" and "Discovering Play and Uti-lizing Play Spaces", two overarching movement fields are added (MSW NRW 2014). Overall, this addresses different degrees of regulation of movement activities, which correlate with the degrees of freedom of play-ing ("play, games, sports") by Sutton-Smith (1978). **Teaching topics** arise by addressing subject-specific content from a specific pedagogical perspec-tive. The guidelines and curricula of all federal states usually provide for six **pedagogical perspectives** that each highlight a specific focus of move-ment activities (see Fig. 3.3).

With this pedagogical interpretation of sports, the subject can make a specific contribution to the general **educational and formation mandate** of the school. Accordingly, in addition to subject-specific goals, contribu-tions of school sports to cross-curricular **tasks of the school** are mentioned, e.g. traffic education, health promotion, intercultural education, political education, aesthetic education or reflective coeducation (MSWWF NRW 1999). In fact, the integration of "intra-subject" and "extra-subject" jus-tifications has now prevailed in the majority of guidelines and curricula in Germany (cf. Prohl 2022). At the same time, the explicitly pedagogi-cal focus of school sports was put back into question with the recent turn towards competence-oriented core curricula. With the output orientation comes the necessity of operationalizing competence expectations, which ultimately led to a stronger orientation towards motor skills and abilities that are easier to measure than overarching competences (cf. Pfitzner and Pürgstaller 2022).

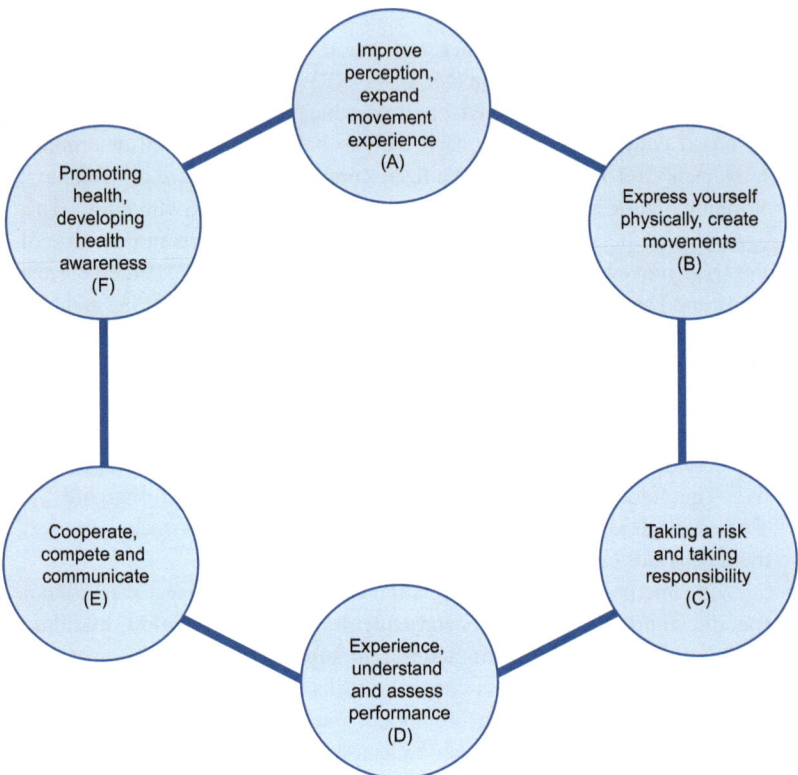

Fig. 3.3 Pedagogical perspectives on sports. (Own illustration)

Sports pedagogical action has so far been almost exclusively understood as an intentional process, in the course of which "educators" systematically influence the behavior of "pupils" in the sense of "teaching". Interestingly, this school pedagogical argument is also taken up in the extracurricular field. Thus, Baur and Braun (2000) conceive the **Pedagogical of youth work in sports** as education for and through sports. Also, corresponding overviews of children's and youth sports take up the idea of a double educational mandate in sports (Brandl-Bredenbeck et al. 2006). This transfers the figure of an intentional, educational sports instruction to extracurricular sports. The discussion about the **change of the education system** has already shown a comprehensive understanding of education with formal, non-formal and informal learning processes since the mid-2000s, which goes far beyond a purely intentional understanding (see Sect. 2.3.3). This complex understanding of education becomes clear in the debate about the learning locations of children and young people.

3.3.4 Learning Locations for Children and Adolescents in Sports

In addition to pedagogical staging, the **framework conditions** of an action field are crucial for what and how children and young people can learn at a location. Based on further education research, a learning location in the *narrower* sense is understood as an educational institution, such as a daycare center, school or university, that organizes educational offers.

▶ **Learning location** In a *broader* sense, it includes "all spatial units that pedagogically stimulate learners—both in the context of formally organized institutions and in the context of informal learning processes" (Tippelt and Reich-Claasen 2010, p. 11). A learning location does not necessarily have to be associated with pedagogical objectives, it is sufficient if it has a learning-stimulating effect.

To differentiate **learning locations for children and adolescents in sports**, the complex concept of education from the post-PISA debate is referred to (see Sect. 2.3.3). However, the model is expanded here to include the area of informal learning locations, so that **formal, non-formal and informal framework conditions** are differentiated on a horizontal level. Formal settings include daycare centers and schools, non-formal ones include sports clubs and youth welfare. The all-day school with its formal and non-formal parts lies in between. Family, informal sports and commercial sports are essentially characterized by informal framework conditions. On a vertical level, a distinction is also made between **formal and informal educational processes** (Neuber and Golenia 2021). Ultimately, it depends on the specific offer, but physical education is usually understood as a formal sports offer in a formal setting, while informal sports are generally seen as an informal educational process in an informal setting (see Fig. 3.4). The following outlines six central learning locations for children and adolescents in sports.

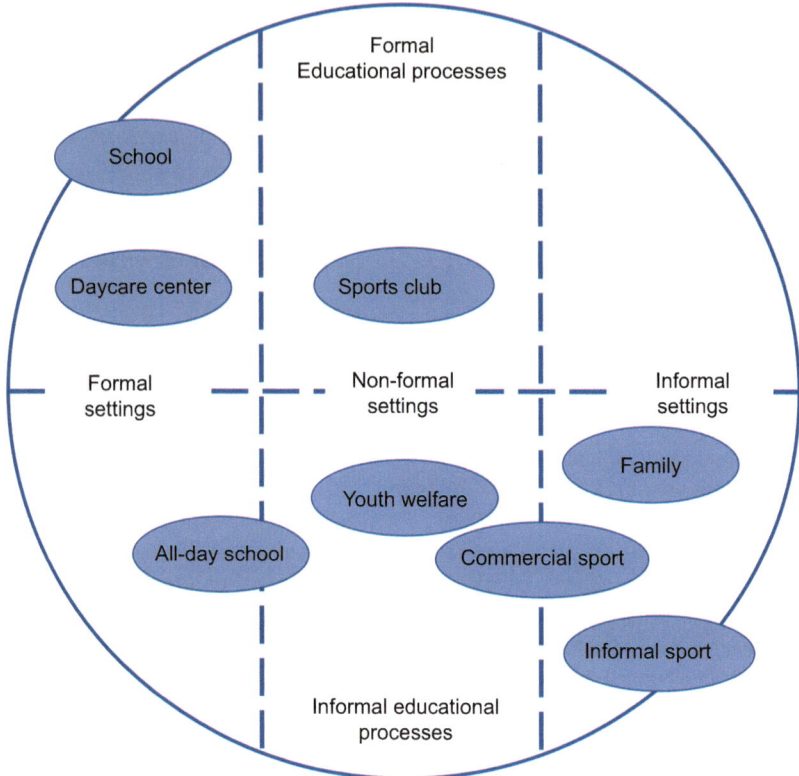

Fig. 3.4 Learning locations for children and young people in sports. (Mod. according to Neuber and Golenia 2021, p. 68)

- The **family** not only forms a central living environment for children and young people, it is also an important learning location. In the pre-school age, parents initially take over the education of their children almost exclusively. They are not only the legal guardians, but they also represent the decisive instance for the development, education and personality formation of their children (cf. Schneewind 2008). As they get older, other reference persons become important, but the family remains one of the most important learning locations for young people until adolescence. This also applies to the field of movement, games and sports. Studies show that the parental home has a central importance for the taking up of physical activities (cf. Züchner 2013). The movement-related learning and educational potential of the family is of great importance overall.

- After the **kindergarten** was initially often understood as a care facility, it has been following a legal educational and educational mandate at least since the 1990s. Conceptually, a turn "from function- and skill-oriented approaches to situation- and child-oriented concepts has taken place" (Zimmer 2020, p. 130). Open offers that encourage experimentation and play have since been at the forefront of elementary pedagogical work. Against this background, the learning and educational potential of the kindergarten is formally framed and can also be formally oriented in the course of guided offers. Nevertheless, it can be assumed that many informal educational processes take place in the kindergarten everyday life within the framework of movement, games and sports activities (cf. Heim 2008).
- After kindergarten, the **school** is the second formal educational institution for children and adolescents. The overarching tasks of the school include the cultivation of culture, the transmission of values and norms, the individual promotion of all students and the preparation for coping with everyday life (cf. Haug 2019). In the school's subject canon, physical education " is the third largest subject after German and mathematics. In addition to physical education, school sports also include extracurricular offers as well as offers for learning with movement in classroom teaching (cf. Scheid 2022). The school reaches all adolescents of an age group, so its sports-related learning and educational potential should be considerable. However, it is also a mandatory educational institution, which can lead to an ambivalent situation for the learners (see section 3.3.3).
- The expansion of the **all-day school** at the beginning of the 2000s is due to the poor results of German students in school aptitude tests ("PISA shock") (see Sect. 2.3.4). Accordingly, it pursues ambitious objectives, such as the individual promotion of all students, a changed learning culture or equal opportunities in the education system (Rauschenbach et al. 2012). In addition to open movement offers during breaks, sport-specific all-day sports offers, especially ball games, are very popular. But there are also cross-cutting offers such as movement promotion, adventure and experience sports or psychomotor skills (cf. Neuber et al. 2015). The learning and educational potential is strongly influenced by the formal framework conditions of the school. Nevertheless, many informal learning opportunities should offer a good alternative to graded physical education.

- The **sports club** is a volunteer organization where people come together who want to do sports together (cf. Baur and Braun 2001). The vast majority of sports clubs are recognized as non-profit and pursue social, cultural and socio-political goals, such as the "promotion of sports" or the "promotion of youth" (Heinemann 2004). Children and adolescents see the club as a place "where their sporting interests are taken into account, their sporting ambitions are supported and their sporting performances are systematically improved" (Brettschneider 2003, p. 28). In addition, it is a place for them for social contacts, sociability and commitment. From its framing, the sports club is a classic non-formal learning place. Its learning and educational potential is also predominantly non-formal, in addition to formal training and informal learning opportunities (cf. Neuber 2021a).
- The field of **child and youth welfare** is wide: In addition to assistance for upbringing, youth social work or child and youth protection, it also refers to extracurricular youth work. Offers of youth work should "tie in with the interests of young people and be co-determined and co-designed by them, enable them to self-determination and encourage and lead them to social responsibility and social commitment" (KJHG, § 11,1). Opportunities for sports-related youth work exist, for example, in the "everyday practices" of child and youth welfare, in sports clubs as carriers of child and youth welfare, in sports-oriented offers of youth social work as well as in youth welfare in the context of fan scenes/fan projects (Derecik and Züchner 2015). The learning place is classically non-formal, but especially in open youth work it should also offer a high informal learning and educational potential (cf. Thole 2016).
- The term **informal sports** refers to movement and sports activities that are self-organized in leisure time. They can be incorporated into everyday life at self-defined times and take place at self-chosen locations. Children mainly engage in everyday cultural activities such as cycling, skating, or swimming (cf. Schmidt 2015). Adolescents also pursue informal play activities and fitness-oriented activities (cf. Bindel 2017). Within movement scenes, complex social negotiation processes also take place, which can lead to the reinterpretation of public spaces (cf. Schwier and Erhorn 2015). The learning and educational potential of informal sports activities lies in the informal framing—precisely because no pedagogical goals are explicitly pursued, spontaneous informal learning opportunities can arise.
- The term **commercial sports offerings** is a collective term for a wide variety of movement and sports offerings that are provided by organizations or individuals as a service with the intention of making a profit (cf. Thieme 2015).

The spectrum of commercial offerings has significantly increased in the past two to three decades. Basically, fitness studios, movement-oriented services, such as dance, tennis, or martial arts schools, as well as infrastructure offerings, such as indoor playgrounds, climbing halls, or high ropes courses can be distinguished (cf. Thieme 2015). The learning and educational potential of commercial sports offerings lies in the fact that they are usually voluntarily chosen by young people and can often also be practiced independently.

3.4   Overview of Pedagogical Basics

The pedagogical foundations are among the general prerequisites for physical education. They form the **pedagogical framework,** within which movement, game, and sports offerings for children and adolescents take place (see Fig. 3.5). Pedagogical action is fundamentally uncertain and ambivalent. It cannot be planned down to the last detail. Therefore, pedagogical stagings always require a reflected justification, which can be quite diverse and should not be limited to simple patterns, such as motor performance. Sport is an **ambivalent**

Fig. 3.5 Overview of pedagogical foundations. (Own illustration)

field of action, which, among other things, due to its high openness and authenticity, offers great pedagogical potential, but can also lead to disregard and exclusion. Therefore, sports pedagogical action is associated with high responsibility. It is commonly understood as education for and through sport in the sense of an **educational physical education.** However, sports activities can also have a pedagogical effect at extracurricular learning locations, even if they do not pursue pedagogical goals. **Movement, games, and sports offerings** for children and adolescents take place under these complex, partly contradictory pedagogical framework conditions and must be staged against this background.

Reflection Questions

1. What are the focal points of sports pedagogical and sports didactic thinking and action?
2. Why is the relationship between "educator" and "pupil" fundamentally asymmetrically structured?
3. What distinguishes the basic forms of (sports) pedagogical action?
4. Why is sport for children and adolescents a fundamentally ambivalent field of action?
5. To what extent does sport offer specific, non-exchangeable learning opportunities that distinguish it from other fields?
6. What patterns of justification can be used for a pedagogical staging of sports?
7. What is the relationship between education for and through sport and movement-related educational processes?
8. On what pedagogical ideas is the concept of educational physical education based?
9. How can learning locations for children and adolescents in sport be characterized?
10. To what extent can learning locations that do not per se pursue pedagogical goals have a pedagogical effect?

References

Balz, E., Reuker, S., Scheid, V., & Sygusch, R. (Eds.). (2022). *Sportpädagogik – Eine Grundlegung.* Stuttgart: Kohlhammer.
Baur, J., & Braun, S. (2000). Über das Pädagogische einer Jugendarbeit im Sport. *Deutsche Jugend, 48*(9), 378–386.

Beckers, E. (1993). Bewegungskultur – Kultur und Bewegung. In E. Beckers & H. Schulz (Eds.), *Sport – Bewegung – Kultur. Auf der Suche nach neuen Bewegungserfahrungen schweift der Blick auch zu fremden Kulturen* (pp. 10–38). Bielefeld: Mane Huchler Medienproduktion.

Beckers, E. (2000). Grundlagen eines erziehenden Sportunterrichts. In Landesinstitut für Schule und Weiterbildung NRW (Eds.), *Erziehender Schulsport. Pädagogische Grundlagen der Curriculumrevision in Nordrhein-Westfalen* (pp. 86–97). Bönen: Verlag für Schule und Weiterbildung.

Beckers, E. (2009). Sportpädagogik und Erziehungswissenschaft. In H. Haag & A. Hummel (Eds.), *Handbuch Sportpädagogik* (2., erweiterte Aufl., pp. 25–34). Schorndorf: Hofmann.

Bildungskommission NRW (Eds.). (1995). *Zukunft der Bildung – Schule der Zukunft* (Denkschrift der Kommission beim Ministerpräsidenten des Landes Nordrhein-Westfalen). Neuwied, Kriftel, Berlin: Luchterhand.

Bindel, T. (2017). Informeller Jugendsport – institutionelle Inanspruchnahme und Wandel eines deutungsoffenen Geschehens. *Diskurs Kindheits- und Jugendforschung, 12*(4), 417–426.

Boriss, K. (2015). *Lernen und Bewegung im Kontext der individuellen Förderung – Förderung exekutiver Funktionen in der Sekundarstufe I* (Bildung und Sport, 8). Wiesbaden: Springer VS.

Brandl-Bredenbeck, H. P., Brettschneider, W.-D., Gerlach, E., & Hofmann, J. (2006). Kinder- und Jugendsport. In H. Haag & B. Strauß (Eds.), *Themenfelder der Sportwissenschaft* (pp. 113–129). Schorndorf: Hofmann.

Brettschneider, W.-D. (2003). Zukunftsfähige Jugendarbeit im Sportverein – Chancen und Grenzen. In N. Neuber (Eds.), *Jugendarbeit im Sport. Ein Handbuch für die Vereinspraxis* (pp. 27–40). Duisburg: Sportjugend NRW.

Breuer, C., Joisten, C., & Schmidt, W. (Eds.). (2020). *Vierter Deutscher Kinder- und Jugendsportbericht – Gesundheit, Leistung, Gesellschaft*. Schorndorf: Hofmann.

Brezinka, W. (1990). *Grundbegriffe der Erziehungswissenschaft*. München: Reinhardt.

Brodtmann, D. (2008). Gesundheitsförderung im Schulsport. In D. Kuhlmann & E. Balz (Eds.), *Sportpädagogik: Ein Arbeitstextbuch* (pp. 180–200). Hamburg: Czwalina.

Derecik, A., & Züchner, I. (2015). Sport in der Kinder- und Jugendhilfe. In W. Schmidt, N. Neuber, T. Rauschenbach, H. P. Brandl-Bredenbeck, J. Süßenbach & C. Breuer (Eds.), *Dritter Deutscher Kinder- und Jugendsportbericht. Kinder- und Jugendsport im Umbruch* (pp. 217–236). Schorndorf: Hofmann.

Fritsch, U. (2007). Ästhetische Erziehung. In R. Laging (Eds.), *Neues Taschenbuch des Sportunterrichts. Kompaktausgabe* (3., veränderte und korrigierte Aufl., pp. 36–46). Hohengehren: Schneider.

Funke-Wieneke, J. (Eds.). (1997). *Vermitteln zwischen Kind und Sache. Erläuterungen zur Sportpädagogik*. Seelze-Velber: Kallmeyer.

Funke-Wieneke, J. (1999). Erziehen im Sportunterricht. *Sportpädagogik, 23*(4), 13–21.

Grimminger, E. (2015). Missachtungsprozesse unter Schülerinnen und Schülern im Sportunterricht – Sportdidaktische Konsequenzen aus einem multimethodischen Forschungsprojekt. *Sportpädagogik, 39*(1), 40–43.

Grupe, O. (1985). Anthropologische Grundfragen der Sportpädagogik. In E. Meinberg, H. Denk & G. Hecker (Eds.), *Texte zur Sportpädagogik* (Texte, Quellen, Dokumente zur Sportwissenschaft, 19, pp. 35–61). Schorndorf: Hofmann.

Haug, A. (2019). Schule als Sozialisationsinstanz. In G. Bovet & V. Huwendiek (Eds.), *Leitfaden Schulpraxis – Pädagogik und Psychologie für den Lehrberuf* (11. edn., pp. 553–572). Berlin: Cornelsen.

Heim, R. (2008). Bewegung, Spiel und Sport im Kontext von Bildung. In W. Schmidt (Eds.), *Zweiter Deutscher Kinder- und Jugendsportbericht. Schwerpunkt: Kindheit* (pp. 21–42). Schorndorf: Hofmann.

Heinemann, K. (1989). Der „nicht-sportliche" Sport. In K. Dietrich & K. Heinemann (Eds.), *Der nicht-sportliche Sport – Beiträge zum Wandel im Sport* (pp. 11–28). Schorndorf: Hofmann.

Heinemann, K. (2004). *Sportorganisationen verstehen und gestalten*. Schorndorf: Hofmann.

Heitger, M. (1999). Erziehung. In G. Reinhold, G. Pollak, & H. Heim (Eds.), *Pädagogik-Lexikon* (pp. 139–144). München: Oldenbourg.

Helsper, W. (1996). Antinomien des Lehrerhandelns in modernisierten pädagogischen Kulturen – Paradoxe Verwendungsweisen von Autonomie und Selbstverantwortlichkeit. In A. Combe & W. Helsper (Eds.), *Pädagogische Professionalität – Untersuchungen zum Typus pädagogischen Handelns* (pp. 521–569). Frankfurt/M.: Suhrkamp.

Helsper, W. (2010). Pädagogisches Handeln in den Antinomien der Moderne. In H.-H. Krüger & W. Helsper (Eds.), *Einführung in Grundbegriffe und Grundfragen der Erziehungswissenschaft* (9. edn., pp. 15–34). Wiesbaden: VS.

Hildebrandt, R. (1993). Lebensweltbezug – Leitmotiv für eine Neuorientierung der Bewegungserziehung in der Grundschule. *Sportwissenschaft, 23,* 259–275.

Hurrelmann, K., & Quenzel, G. (2016). *Lebensphase Jugend – Eine Einführung in die sozialwissenschaftliche Jugendforschung* (13. überarbeitete Aufl.). Weinheim, Basel: Beltz Juventa.

Idel, T.-S., & Ulrich, H. (Eds.). (2017). *Handbuch Reformpädagogik*. Weinheim: Beltz.

KJHG (Kinder- und Jugendhilfegesetz). *Sozialgesetzbuch (SGB). Achtes Buch (VIII). Kinder- und Jugendhilfe. 11 SGB VIII Jugendarbeit.* Accessed 03.04.2018 http://www.sozialgesetzbuch-sgb.de/sgbviii/11.html.

Krüger, H.-H., & Helsper, W. (Eds.). (2010). *Einführung in Grundbegriffe und Grundfragen der Erziehungswissenschaft* (9. edn.). Wiesbaden: VS.

Laging, R. (2017). *Bewegung in Schule und Unterricht – Anregungen für eine bewegungsorientierte Schulentwicklung*. Stuttgart: Kohlhammer.

Litt, T. (1963). *Naturwissenschaft und Menschenbildung* (4. edn.). Heidelberg: Quelle & Meyer.

Luhmann, N., & Schorr, K. E. (1982). Das Technologiedefizit der Erziehung und die Pädagogik. In N. Luhmann & K. E. Schorr (Eds.), *Zwischen Technologie und Selbstreferenz. Fragen an die Pädagogik* (pp. 11–41). Berlin: Suhrkamp.

Meinberg, E. (1984). *Kinderhochleistungssport: Fremdbestimmung oder Selbstentfaltung? Pädagogische, anthropologische und ethische Orientierungen*. Köln: Strauß.

Meinberg, E. (1996). *Hauptprobleme der Sportpädagogik. Eine Einführung* (3. edn.). Darmstadt: Wissenschaftliche Buchgesellschaft.

MSW NRW (Ministerium für Schule und Weiterbildung des Landes Nordrhein-Westfalen). (2014). *Rahmenvorgaben für den Schulsport in Nordrhein-Westfalen*. Düsseldorf: MSW.

MSWWF NRW (Ministerium für Schule und Weiterbildung, Wissenschaft und Forschung des Landes Nordrhein-Westfalen). (Eds.). (1999). *Sekundarstufe II – Gymnasium/Gesamtschule. Richtlinien und Lehrpläne*. Düsseldorf: MSWWF.

Neuber, N. (2007). *Entwicklungsförderung im Jugendalter. Theoretische Grundlagen und empirische Befunde aus sportpädagogischer Perspektive*. Schorndorf: Hofmann.

Neuber, N. (2020). *Fachdidaktische Konzepte Sport – Zielgruppen und Voraussetzungen* (Basiswissen Lernen im Sport). Wiesbaden: Springer VS. https://doi.org/10.1007/978-3-658-28464-0.

Neuber, N. (Eds.). (2021a). *Kinder- und Jugendsportforschung in Deutschland – Bilanz und Perspektive* (Bildung und Sport, 26). Wiesbaden: Springer VS. https://doi.org/10.1007/978-3-658-30776-9.

Neuber, N. (2021b). *Fachdidaktische Konzepte Sport II – Themenfelder und Perspektiven* (Basiswissen Lernen im Sport). Wiesbaden: Springer VS. https://doi.org/10.1007/978-3-658-30249-8.

Neuber, N., & Gebken, U. (2009). Anerkennung als sportpädagogischer Begriff – eine thematische Einführung. In U. Gebken & N. Neuber (Eds.), *Anerkennung als sportpädagogischer Begriff* (Jahrbuch Bewegungs- und Sportpädagogik in Theorie und Forschung, 8, pp. 7–18). Hohengehren: Schneider.

Neuber, N., Kaufmann, N., & Salomon, S. (2015). Ganztag und Sport. In W. Schmidt, N. Neuber, T. Rauschenbach, H. P. Brandl-Bredenbeck, J. Süßenbach & C. Breuer (Eds.), *Dritter Deutscher Kinder- und Jugendsportbericht. Kinder- und Jugendsport im Umbruch* (pp. 416–443). Schorndorf: Hofmann.

Neuber N., & Golenia, M. (2021). Lernorte für Kinder und Jugendliche im Sport. In A. Güllich & M. Krüger (Eds.), *Sport in Kultur und Gesellschaft – Handbuch Sport und Sportwissenschaft* (pp. 55–71). Berlin, Heidelberg: Springer.

Neuber, N., & Scheid, V. (2021). Entwicklungstheoretische Ansätze. In E. Balz, S. Reuker, V. Scheid & R. Sygusch (Eds.), *Sportpädagogik – Eine Grundlegung* (pp. 77–89). Stuttgart: Kohlhammer.

Nohl, H. (1963). *Die pädagogische Bewegung in Deutschland und ihre Theorie* (6. edn.). Frankfurt/M.: Schulte-Bulmke.

Oelkers, J. (2001). Theorien der Erziehung – Erziehung als historisches und aktuelles Problem. In L. Roth (Eds.), *Pädagogik – Handbuch für Studium und Praxis* (2. edn., pp. 266–276). München: Oldenbourg.

Pfitzner, M., & Neuber, N. (2012). Individuelle Förderung im Sport – Didaktisch-methodische Grundlagen. In N. Neuber & M. Pfitzner (Eds.), *Individuelle Förderung im Sport – Pädagogische Grundlagen und didaktisch-methodische Konzepte* (Begabungsforschung, 14, pp. 75–95). Münster: Lit.

Pfitzner, M., Neuber, N., Eckenbach, K., Liersch, J., Ludwig, K., & Aschebrock, K. (2021). Lernförderung durch Bewegung – Die Auswirkungen von Bewegung auf das exekutive System und Potenziale für einen lernförderlichen Sportunterricht. *Sportpädagogik*, *45*(1), 2–8.

Pfitzner, M., & Pürgstaller, E. (2022). Lehren, Lernen und Unterrichten im Sport – Sportdidaktik. In A. Güllich & M. Krüger (Eds.), *Sport – Das Lehrbuch für das Sportstudium* (pp. 529–561). Berlin: Springer Spektrum. https://doi.org/10.1007/978-3-662-64695-3_14.

Prohl, R. (2010). *Grundriss der Sportpädagogik* (3. edn.). Wiebelsheim: Limpert.

Prohl, R. (2022). Der Doppelauftrag des Erziehenden Sportunterrichts. In V. Scheid & R. Prohl (Eds.), *Sportdidaktik – Grundlagen, Vermittlungsformen, Bewegungsfelder* (3., durchgesehene und korrigierte Aufl., pp. 64–84). Wiebelsheim: Limpert.

Prohl, R., & Scheid, V. (2022). Zum Verhältnis zwischen Sportpädagogik und Sportdidaktik. In V. Scheid & R. Prohl (Eds.), *Sportdidaktik – Grundlagen, Vermittlungsformen, Bewegungsfelder* (3., durchgesehene und korrigierte Aufl., pp. 10–14). Wiebelsheim: Limpert.

Rauschenbach, T., Arnoldt, B., Steiner, C., & Stolz, H.-J. (2012). *Ganztagsschule als Hoffnungsträger für die Zukunft? Ein Reformprojekt auf dem Prüfstand. Expertise des Deutschen Jugendinstituts (DJI) im Auftrag der Bertelsmann Stiftung.* Gütersloh: Bertelsmann Stiftung.

Rogers, C. (1989). *Freiheit und Engagement. Personzentriertes Lehren und Lernen.* Geist und Psyche. Frankfurt a. M: Fischer.

Scheid, V. (2022). Organisationsformen und Akteure des Schulsports. In V. Scheid & R. Prohl (Eds.), *Sportdidaktik – Grundlagen, Vermittlungsformen, Bewegungsfelder* (3., durchgesehene und korrigierte Aufl., pp. 31–48). Wiebelsheim: Limpert.

Scheid, V., & Prohl, R. (Eds.). (2022). *Sportdidaktik – Grundlagen, Vermittlungsformen, Bewegungsfelder* (3., durchgesehene und korrigierte Aufl., pp. 31–48). Wiebelsheim: Limpert.

Scheid V., & Oesterhelt, V. (2022). Grundbegriff der Sportpädagogik. In E. Balz, S. Reuker, V. Scheid & R. Sygusch (Eds.), *Sportpädagogik – Eine Grundlegung* (pp. 17–32). Stuttgart: Kohlhammer.

Scherler, K. (1997). Die Instrumentalisierungsdebatte in der Sportpädagogik. *Sportpädagogik, 21*(2), 5–11.

Schmidt, W. (2015). Informeller Sport. In W. Schmidt, N. Neuber, T. Rauschenbach, H. P. Brandl-Bredenbeck, J. Süßenbach & C. Breuer (Eds.), *Dritter Deutscher Kinder- und Jugendsportbericht. Kinder- und Jugendsport im Umbruch* (pp. 201–216). Schorndorf: Hofmann.

Schmidt, W., Neuber, N., Rauschenbach, T., Brandl-Bredenbeck, H.-P., Süßenbach, J., & Breuer, C. (Eds.). (2015). *Dritter Deutscher Kinder- und Jugendsportbericht: Kinder- und Jugendsport im Umbruch.* Schorndorf: Hofmann.

Schmidt, S. C. E., Burchartz, A., Kolb, S., Niessner, C., Oriwol, D., Hanssen-Doose, A., Worth, A., & Woll, A. (2021). Zur Situation der körperlich-sportlichen Aktivität von Kindern und Jugendlichen während der Covid-19 Pandemie in Deutschland: Die Motorik-Modul Studie (MoMo). *KIT Scientific Working Papers, 165*, 1–17.

Schneewind, K. A. (2008). Sozialisation in der Familie. In K. Hurrelmann, M. Grundmann & S. Walper (Eds.), *Handbuch Sozialisationsforschung* (7., vollständig überarbeitete Aufl., pp. 256–273). Weinheim, Basel: Beltz.

Schwier J., & Erhorn, J. (2015). Trendsport. In W. Schmidt, N. Neuber, T. Rauschenbach, H. P. Brandl-Bredenbeck, J. Süßenbach & C. Breuer (Eds.), *Dritter Deutscher Kinder- und Jugendsportbericht. Kinder- und Jugendsport im Umbruch* (pp. 179–200). Schorndorf: Hofmann.

Sutton-Smith, B. (1978). *Die Dialektik des Spiels.* Schorndorf: Hofmann.

Tausch, R., & Tausch, A.-M. (1998). *Erziehungs-Psychologie. Begegnung von Person zu Person* (11. edn.). Göttingen: Hogrefe.

Thieme, L. (2015). Kommerzieller Sport. In W. Schmidt, N. Neuber, T. Rauschenbach, H. P. Brandl-Bredenbeck, J. Süßenbach & C. Breuer (Eds.), *Dritter Deutscher Kinder- und Jugendsportbericht. Kinder- und Jugendsport im Umbruch* (pp. 162–178). Schorndorf: Hofmann.

Thole, W. (2016). Non-formales und informelles Lernen in der Kinder- und Jugendhilfe. In T. Burger, M. Harring & M. Witte (Eds.), *Handbuch informelles Lernen – Interdisziplinäre und internationale Perspektiven* (pp. 439–459). Weinheim, Basel: Beltz Juventa.

Tiemann, H. (2015). Inklusiven Sportunterricht gestalten – didaktisch methodische Überlegungen. In M. Giese (Eds.), *Inklusiver Sportunterricht in Theorie und Praxis* (Edition Schulsport, 27, pp. 53–66). Aachen: Meyer & Meyer.

Tippelt, R., & Reich-Claasen, J. (2010). Lernorte – Organisationale und lebensweltbezogene Perspektiven. *REPORT Zeitschrift für Weiterbildungsforschung, 2*, 11–21.

Trenz, G. (2019). Interaktionsprozesse im Unterricht. In G. Bovet & V. Huwendiek (Eds.), *Leitfaden Schulpraxis – Pädagogik und Psychologie für den Lehrberuf* (11. edn., pp. 396–420). Berlin: Cornelsen.

Zimmer, R. (2019). *Handbuch Psychomotorik. Theorie und Praxis der psychomotorischen Förderung von Kindern* (1. edn.). Freiburg: Herder.

Zimmer, R. (2020). *Handbuch Bewegungserziehung – Grundlagen für Ausbildung und pädagogische Praxis* (26. Überarbeitete Aufl.). Freiburg: Herder.

Zinnecker, J. (1991). Jugend als Bildungsmoratorium. Zur Theorie des Wandels der Jugendphase in west- und osteuropäischen Gesellschaften. In W. Melzer, W. Heitmeyer, L. Liegle & J. Zinnecker (Eds.), *Osteuropäische Jugend im Wandel. Ergebnisse vergleichender Jugendforschung in der Sowjetunion, Polen, Ungarn und der ehemaligen DDR* (pp. 9–25). Weinheim: Juventa.

Züchner, I. (2013). Sportliche Aktivitäten im Aufwachsen junger Menschen. In M. Grgic & I. Züchner (Eds.), *Medien, Kultur und Sport. Was Kinder und Jugendliche machen und ihnen wichtig ist. Die MediKuS-Studie* (pp. 89–138). Weinheim, Basel: Beltz Juventa.

Didactic Models

4

Abstract

This chapter deals with didactic models for teaching and physical education. Based on considerations about the complexity of teaching processes, four general didactic models are presented: the educational -theoretical didactics, the learning -theoretical didactics, the communicative didactics, and the constructivist didactics. Building on this, four sport didactic models are described: the planning didactics, the implementation didactics, the evaluation didactics, and the competence-oriented didactics. An excursion into precursors of sports didactic models complements the chapter.

4.1   Introduction

General and subject-specific **models and concepts** are intended to provide basic orientations for the theoretical and practical examination of teaching-learning processes in sports. At its core, it is about understanding teaching in general and physical education in particular. All sports didactic approaches share the conviction that movement, game, and sports offers for children and adolescents can be pedagogically staged. In accordance with the subject culture, the considerations mainly refer to **sports in school** (Neuber 2020, pp. 137–158). After German and mathematics, sports is the third largest subject taught. School sports have both intra-school and extra-school tasks. In the sense of educational physical education, these tasks can be justified as subject-immanent *(education for sports)* and cross-curricular goals *(education through sports)* (Prohl 2022). Therefore,

© The Author(s), under exclusive license to Springer Fachmedien Wiesbaden   59
Gmbh, part of Springer Nature 2025
N. Neuber, *Didactics of Physical Education and Sport*,
https://doi.org/10.1007/978-3-658-47188-0_4

education and formation can be highlighted as central tasks of pedagogical action within the framework of **educational physical education** (see Sect. 3.3.3).

Physical education takes place under complex conditions. The paradoxical tension of the three **functions of school** (Haug 2019)—qualification, selection, and integration—is extended by at least one level in physical education. In addition to the basic contradiction between qualification and selection, there is the contradiction between "sports as subjective fulfillment of meaning," as many children and adolescents appreciate outside of school, and sports as a "mandatory school event," which is subject to school curricula and obligations. Prohl (2010, p. 100) calls this the **double paradox of physical education** (see Fig. 4.1). Pedagogical tasks and school conditions require that (prospective) PE teachers orient themselves and become aware of their own position in order to act justifiably. Sports didactics offer sports didactic **models and concepts** for this, which are presented in this and the following chapter. The introduction and basic terms are the same in both chapters (see Chap. 5). *Specific* subject-didactic concepts of *medium* range are presented elsewhere (Neuber 2020, 2021).

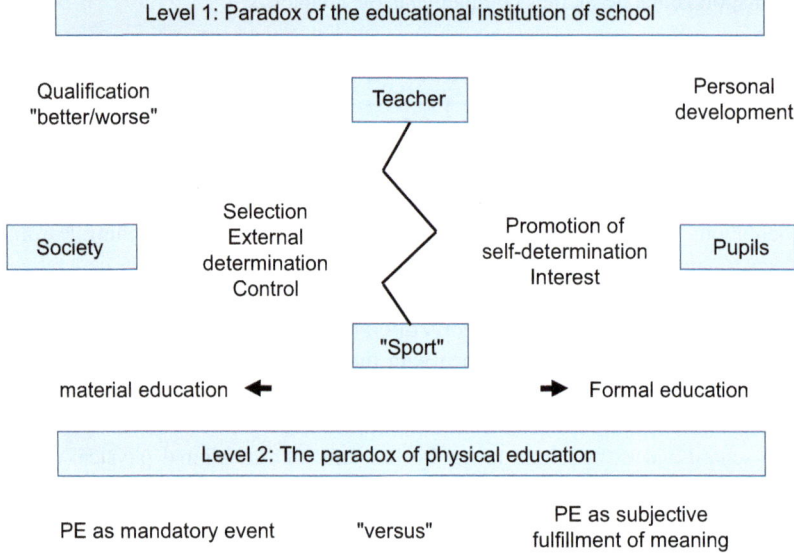

Fig. 4.1 Double paradox of physical education. (Mod. according to Prohl, 2010, p. 100)

4.2 Basic Concepts

The basic concepts of didactic models and concepts initially include "instruction" and "instructioning".

▶ **Instruction** is the targeted planning, implementation, and evaluation of teaching-learning processes in an institutional context.

Instructioning is the activity of professional teachers, which is "more strongly tied to the transmission of content that the teacher masters and should convey in such a way that it can be learned by learners who do not yet understand it" (Helsper and Keuffer 2010, p. 92). The **didactics** is the science of instruction and instructioning (cf. Huwendiek 2019). These considerations can be applied to the subject of pyhsical education.

▶ **Physical education** is then the targeted planning, implementation, and evaluation of teaching-learning processes in the field of movement, games, and sports in an institutional context.

Teaching pyhsical education is the professional pedagogical activity of PE teachers, which aims at initiating teaching-learning processes in the field of movement, games, and sports. **Sports didactics** is the science of physical education and teaching pyhsical education. While "pyhsical education" focuses more on the structures of the teaching-learning activity, "teaching physical education" refers to the process of implementation (Scherler 2008, pp. 13–17).

The basic structures of instructional action are summarized in didactic models and concepts. A conceptual starting point is the **didactic triangle,** which describes the mutual relationships between "teacher", "student", and "subject matter" (Huwendiek 2019, p. 34). **Didactic models** are more complex. They can be understood as general "theoretical structures for analysing and modeling of didactic action in school and non-school contexts" (Jank and Meyer 2020, p. 35). In contrast, **didactic concepts** are more implementation-oriented and denote "overall orientations of didactic-methodological action, in which a justified connection of goal, content, and method decisions is established" (Jank and Meyer 2020, p. 305). They define basic principles of teaching and usually also provide concrete suggestions for designing the instrucion (see Chap. 5). The specific interactions of goals, contents, and methods of teaching are referred to as **implication context** (Jank and Meyer 2020, p. 55).

4.3   Foundations

Didactic models attempt to organize the complexity of instructional events at a general level. A simple, well-known basic model is the **didactic triangle** (cf. Fig. 4.2). This describes the mutual relationships between "teacher", "student", and "subject matter" (learning object) (Huwendiek 2019, p. 34). The didactic triangle is often criticized for its simple structure. Thus, Jank and Meyer (2020, p. 55) complain that teaching is thought of as one-sidedly teacher-centered and does not address the methodical action of learners. Nevertheless, the model can represent essential relationships of teaching, such as the task of the teacher to prepare the subject matter in such a way that the students can learn it. Similarly fundamental is the interplay of goals, contents, and methods, which in didactics is referred to as "interdependence" or **implication context**. This means that the three elements must not only be coherent in themselves, but also that there is a suitable interaction between them. If, for example, a goal is changed, contents and methods must necessarily be adapted (Jank and Meyer 2020, pp. 55–60).

A more comprehensive basic model is the **structural model of instruction** by Jank and Meyer (2020, pp. 61–71). It assumes that instruction can be described by the five structural features of goals, content, social relationships, actions, and time (see Fig. 4.3). Each feature is "shaped by its own didactic logic, which must be taken into account in the analysis, planning, and implementation of instruction" (Jank and Meyer 2020, p. 63). In addition, the model is surrounded in an extended form by three "rings" representing the personal, institutional, and societal **prerequisites of instruction** (Jank and Meier 2020, pp. 67–69). The structural model is often used as a starting point for the representation of general and subject-specific models because it describes central elements of instruction. Therefore, it can also be used to analyze the **basic features of physical education**. However, it is not free from normative assumptions. A (theoretical instructional) model is also used in this volume (see Chap. 1), which, of course, is not compatible with all conceptions of instruction and instructional analysis.

Fig. 4.2 Didactic triangle. (Mod. according to Scherler 2008, p. 17)

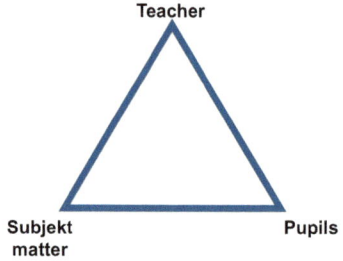

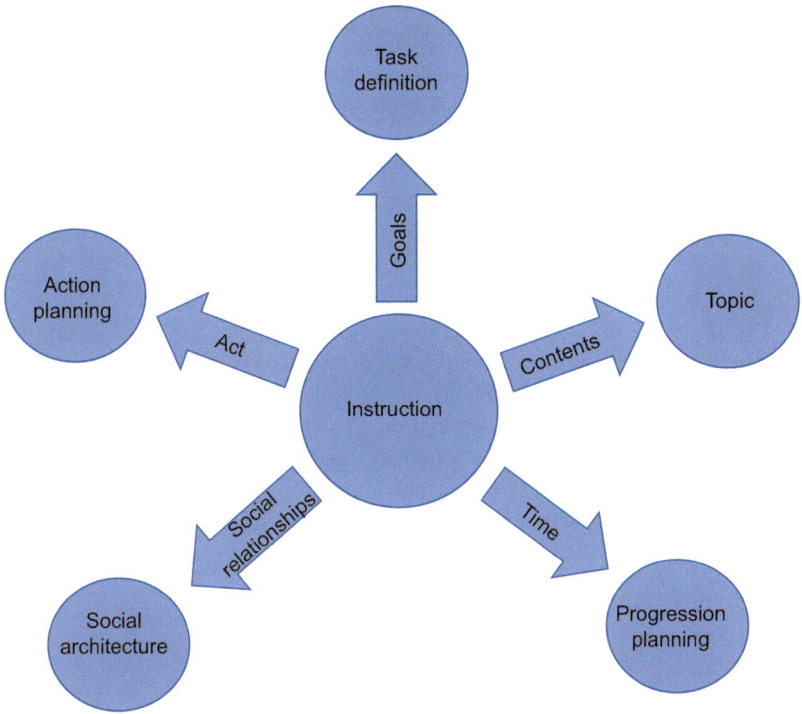

Fig. 4.3 Structural model of instruction. (Mod. according to Jank and Meyer 2020, p. 63)

The complexity of instructional structures and processes is expanded in **physical education** by the movement in space. Teachers and learners are not—as in the classroom—more or less statically in one place, but are constantly in motion. Therefore, the actions of students and teachers in physical education are particularly diverse (Krieger 2011). The **forms of action of learners** include exploring and testing, learning and practicing, training and competing, playing and discovering, improvising and designing, as well as building and constructing. Correspondingly complex are also the **forms of action of teachers** with planning and evaluating, supervising and instructing, observing and correcting, diagnosing and assessing, differentiating and integrating, as well as motivating and disciplining (cf. Wolters et al. 2000). The diversity of forms of action is complemented by the diversity of prerequisites of students, not least because many children and adolescents have prior subject-specific experiences. Therefore, sports is considered a particularly prerequisite-rich subject (Neuber 2020, pp. 93–113).

Against the backdrop of this complexity, Karlheinz Scherler (2008) advocates for a sports-related extension of the didactic triangle (see Fig. 4.4).

▶ The **didactic star** is a basic model in sports didactics, at the center of which is the teacher, who has three essential tasks: the presentation of content, interaction with students, and the organization of the framework conditions.

The latter is to be seen as a specificity, as there is comparatively a lot to be organized in physical education, e.g., sports equipment, spaces, and times. However, the teacher-centered perspective of the model can also be criticized here, not least because the activities of the students are left out. On the other hand, the teacher has the **responsibility for the instruction,** no matter how student-oriented it may be staged. Accordingly, Scherler formulates as a requirement for the actions of teachers that content, organization, and interaction must be coherent and that these "three modes of action [...] must fit together" (Scherler 2008, p. 19). Based

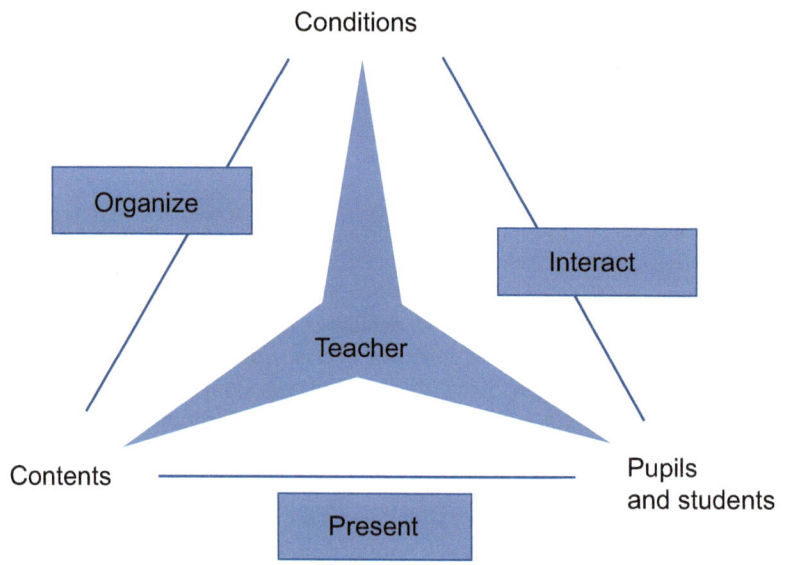

Fig. 4.4   Didactic star. (Mod. according to Scherler 2008, p. 18)

on these basic considerations, selected general didactic and sports didactic models are presented and summarized in a conclusion.

4.3.1 General Didactic Models

A model describes ideal patterns or role models that action should be oriented towards. In an analytical sense, it is understood as "a simplifying, usually graphical representation of complex facts and relationships" (Terhart 2019, p. 148). Accordingly, **models of general didactics** aim to represent fundamental aspects of teaching and learning. They can be understood as educational theory structures that serve the analysis and modeling of didactic action in school and extracurricular fields.

▶ **Didactic models** are intended to "theoretically comprehensively and practically consequential clarify the prerequisites, possibilities, consequences, and limits of teaching and learning" (Jank and Meyer 2020, p. 35). They can usually be assigned to a specific **epistemological basic position**.

Since general didactic models are supposed to apply to all school levels, types of schools, and school subjects, and also to extracurricular fields, they inevitably remain relatively general and formal. Nevertheless, they are supposed to provide an overview and order for the **process of teaching and learning**, reduce complexity, and provide some orientation for action (Jank and Meyer 2020, pp. 35–36). In general didactics, there is a multitude of **didactic models** with very different guiding ideas, theoretical references, and model conceptions. The spectrum ranges from educational theory and learning theory didactics to dialectical and critical-communicative didactics, constructivist didactics, neurodidactics, and educational pathway didactics (cf. Terhart 2021).

▶   **Literature Tip** Terhart, E. (2019). *Didaktik - Eine Einführung.* Stuttgart: Reclam.
         The volume by Ewald Terhart appears in the cost-effective Reclam series and deals with the basics of teaching and learning as well as with didactic theories and models from a general didactic perspective.

In addition, the models are not static, but evolve over time and with the individuals involved. For example, the **learning-theoretical didactics** "from a simple empiricism […] of the 'Berlin School' to an ideology-critical conception at the beginning of the 1970s to very subject-related, partly already quasi-therapeutic forms in the 'Hamburg Model'" has a moving history behind it (Terhart 2019, p. 158). The extent to which didactic models can fulfill the demands placed on them is controversial. Assessments range from "holiday didactics" to "problematisation aids" to the formulation of "teaching recipes" (Jank and Meyer 2020, p. 36). Ultimately, their justification depends on whether they contribute to describing teaching-learning processes from a specific perspective and thus provide an **orientation for teaching action**. In this sense, four selected general didactic models are presented below (see Table 4.1).

The **educational-theoretical didactics** ("Bildungstheoretische Didaktik") is the first major general didactic model of the post-war period. It aims at the "initiation of education through the encounter of young people with culture" (Terhart 2021, p. 30). Material education theories focus on the content of education. Formal education theories emphasize the development of students' abilities and potentials. In the concept of **categorical formation ("Kategoriale Bildung")**, material and formal theories are combined (Klafki 1957). Educational teaching is

Table 4.1 Overview of General Didactic Models

	Educational-theoretical Didactics	**Learning-theoretical Didactics**	**Communicative Didactics**	**Constructivist Didactics**
Representative	Wolfgang Klafki	Paul Heimann	Walter Popp	Kersten Reich
Guiding Idea	Education through the encounter of adolescents with culture	Ordering of structural features for planning instruction	Teaching as a social situation in symmetrical communication	Learning as an act of constructing knowledge in the community
Model Conception	Categorical education as a connection of material and formal education	Interdependence of prerequisite and decision fields	Social interaction processes as the basis of learning	Construction of knowledge
Didactic Method	Didactic analysis in the sense of interpretation and structuring of contents	Structural analysis for the rational organisation of teaching-learning processes	Recourse to the diversity of methodological approaches	Construction, reconstruction, deconstruction of knowledge
Theory Reference	Hermeneutic Science	Empirical-analytical Science	Critical Educational Science	Constructivist Science

attributed to the humanities-hermeneutic pedagogy. At the center of the approach is the **didactic analysis,** i.e., the interpretation and didactic structuring of teaching content. To determine the educational content of subjects, questions are particularly asked about their present significance, future significance, structure, exemplary significance, and accessibility (Jank and Meyer 2020, p. 205). The selection and arrangement of content are therefore in the foreground, while methodological questions are rather subordinate. The content reference becomes particularly clear in the cross-disciplinary formulated "epoch-typical key problems" of Klafki's critical-constructive didactics (1995), such as peace, environment, or democratization.

The **learning-theoretical didactics** ("Lerntheoretische Didaktik") is also one of the classics of general didactic models. At its core, it is about the organization of structural features of teaching in the sense of a goal-oriented lesson planning (Heimann et al. 1965). From the perspective of the acting teacher, the approach tries to provide him with "scientifically secured information for the design of teaching" (Terhart 2021, p. 31). In this respect, learning-theoretical didactics can be attributed to empirical-analytical science. The focus is on the **structural analysis of teaching,** in which, starting from the anthropogenic and sociocultural prerequisites ("prerequisite fields"), intention, content, method, and media selection ("decision fields") are clarified (Jank and Meyer 2020, p. 263). These factors are interdependent and influence the effects of teaching, which in turn are taken as a prerequisite in subsequent planning. Therefore, learning-theoretical models are often represented as a control loop (see Fig. 1.3). Teaching is thus understood less as an educational encounter with the world, but rather as a "purpose-rational and success-controlled **organization of teaching-learning processes**" (Terhart 2019, p. 157).

The **communicative didactics** ("Kommunikative Didaktik") can be understood as a counter-movement to educational and learning-theoretical approaches (Popp 1976). The approach focuses on the process of social interaction in the learning group. Teaching is understood "as a social situation in which the participants bring their respective personal experiences, views, and definitions" (Terhart 2021, p. 33). To this end, communicative didactics draws on both philosophical and communication-theoretical sciences as well as findings from empirical teaching research. However, the focus is less on instruction processes and more on **interaction structures** and their effects. Communicative didactics also aims "at the establishment of as far as possible power-free, symmetrical communication in the classroom" (Terhart 2019, p. 161). This brings it close to **dialectical didactics,** which understands the contradiction between leadership and self-activity as the "driving force" of teaching (Jank and Meyer 2020, p. 248). Both approaches aim to put teaching-learning processes "at eye level". Therefore, it is not surprising that communicative didactics has largely transitioned into concepts of student-oriented, experiential, and open teaching, the variety of methods of which is practically used (Terhart 2021, p. 35).

Among the more recent general didactic models is the **constructivist didactics ("Konstruktivistische Didaktik")**. This approach also focuses on instructional interaction processes (Reich 1997). However, the starting point is the conviction that there is no knowledge "in itself", but that all knowledge is constructed. This means that "learning is an act of **(co-)construction in communities**, that teachers cannot generate learning, but can only stimulate it, and that judging learning outcomes on the basis of right/wrong distinctions is inadequate" (Terhart 2021, p. 36). Therefore, the epistemological reference point of the approach lies in constructivist science. Fundamental to constructivist didactics is the methodological triad of **construction, reconstruction, and deconstruction,** which leads to the triple "unfolding task" of invention, reproduction, and unmasking of knowledge in teaching (Jank and Meyer 2020, pp. 293–297). Learning thus becomes a "co-constructing activity of the learners themselves, with every learning outcome ultimately having to count as a success" (Terhart 2019, pp. 165–166). This makes the approach particularly interesting for more recent concepts of informal learning, networked learning, or digital learning.

4.3.2   Sports Didactic Models

The discussion about didactic models in general didactics is taken up in sports didactics (e.g., Pfitzner 2021), but it does not lead to a larger discussion of *subject-specific* models. At the beginning of the 1970s—in the transition from the theory of physical education to the sports curriculum—this was quite different (see box). Today, the discussion is usually less fundamental. This may have terminological reasons. Thus, Balz (1992, p. 13) concludes that sports didactic "approaches" have a certain proximity to didactic concepts, but ultimately are to be located "somewhere" between didactic models and concepts. On the other hand, the discussion about **teaching and learning in sports** is very complex. Thus, more or less all sub-disciplines of sports science deal with mediation issues, such as training science (e.g., Weineck 2019) or sports psychology (e.g., Hänsel et al. 2022). General **sports didactic discussions** do pick up on more recent theoretical developments. For example, Thiele and Schierz (2011) advocate for a further development of the didactic guiding idea of action competence in the sense of an "action enabling", but remain at a rough draft. Other approaches deal with the question of the **subject matter of sports** and develop alternative models such as the "subject model sports" (Messmer 2013) or the "four-field model of sports"

(Balz 2021). However, they do not provide a comprehensive sports didactic model in the sense of a fundamental analysis of teaching and learning in sports.

Precursors of Sports Didactic Models
Since the origins of Western history in ancient Greece, there have been approaches to a **culture of the body or movement,** which is to be imparted to young people (Krüger 2020). With the beginning of the modern era, these approaches were further developed pedagogically, for example in Rousseau's "natural" education or among the philanthropists, in natural gymnastics or reform pedagogical physical education, but also in the politically motivated physical education of National Socialism (Prohl 2010, pp. 21–88). From the end of the Second World War until about the end of the 1960s, the predominant model was initially the **theory of physical education,** which was then replaced by curriculum theory in the early 1970s. While physical education focused on a pedagogical justification for movement in school, the **sports curriculum** was oriented towards societal changes in sports. This was underpinned by the so-called "realistic turn" in pedagogy. Educational science increasingly saw itself "as a social science, adopted the methods of empirical social research [...] and turned away from pedagogical values and towards pedagogical facts" (Größing 2007, pp. 18–19). Accordingly, physical education became school sports education.

The two precursors of sports didactic models in the post-war period can be understood as ideal-typical for the spectrum of sports didactic orientations. While the **theory of physical education** derived its goals normatively-hermeneutically and selected its content independently of extracurricular developments, the **sports curriculum** was concerned with socially relevant qualifications for extracurricular sports (Pfitzner and Pürgstaller 2022, pp. 531–533). On the one hand, there were methodical master teachings and trust in the success of the lessons, on the other hand, a more or less abstract teaching technology with measurable results and quantitative learning success controls (Prohl 2022, pp. 49–51). In contrast to the supposedly timeless **values and norms** of physical education, the needs of students for extracurricular "sports" should be decisive here (Größing 2007, pp. 18–22). However, the hopes placed in the sports curriculum have not been fulfilled. It soon became apparent that "the student as an individual person threatened to disappear behind the socially determined qualifications and **teaching/learning technologies**" (Prohl 2022, p. 50). Thus, sports didactics continues to debate the right orientations for pyhsical education to this day.

There are indeed two established sports didactic models that meet the demand for complex modeling. The **planning didactics** aims at determining criteria "according to which the diversity of phenomena, situations and structural elements [of sports education in the sense of targeted planning] can be made manageable and ordered" (Größing 2007, p. 38). The **evaluation didactics** focuses on the reflection of real teaching processes with the aim of improving future practice (Scherler 2008). These approaches are complemented by an **implementation didactics**, which takes up the three-step process of planning, implementing and evaluating and tries to design a model for the acute teaching event (Neuber 2004). On the other hand, the discussion about competence-oriented sports education can be used and interpreted in the sense of a **competence-oriented didactics**. Although there is no uniform didactic model here either, there are basic features of sports didactic competence models (Pfitzner 2021, p. 29–32). Thus, four subject-specific models with different guiding ideas and theoretical references can be exemplarily highlighted (see Table 4.2).

The model of **planning didactics** ("Planungsdidaktik") has a tradition in sports didactics (Söll 1996; Größing 2007; Heymen and Leue 2014). It is based on an arrangement of structural features with the aim of comprehensive planning of sports lessons (see Fig. 4.5). It primarily sets in *before* the implementation of sports lessons. As part of the **condition analysis**, the prerequisites of school and society, but also of teachers and learners are questioned ("condition level"). The **structural analysis** attempts to capture as many, ideally all elements of a lesson in order to ensure the smooth running of a lesson. This includes, for example, goals, content, methods, organizational and action forms of a lesson ("decision level"). In the **impact analysis**, the consequences of the lessons are evaluated, e.g. the abilities, knowledge and attitudes of the students ("evaluation level") (Größing 2007, pp. 35–41). Planning didactics aims at the **structural perspective** of teaching and is therefore particularly suitable for "novices of the teaching business" because it provides an overview of relevant aspects of sports lessons from the "top view" (Scherler 2008, pp. 13–15). A reference to general didactics exists primarily with regard to the learning-theoretical model.

A model idea that sets in *during* the implementation of the lesson is the **implementation didactics** ("Durchführungsdidaktik"). The term has not yet established itself, but there are numerous approaches to the concrete implementation of sports lessons in sports didactics (cf. Neuber, 2004). For example, Treutlein (1998) deals with the importance of the relationship level between PE teachers and students in the sense of a **relationship didactics**, which he considers central to the success of sports lessons. Funke-Wieneke (1997) aims in his **mediation didactics** to mediate between the movement task and the efforts of the

Table 4.2 Overview of Sports Didactic Models

	Planning Didactics	Implementation Didactics	Evaluation Didactics	Competence-Oriented Didactics
Representative	Stefan Größing	Nils Neuber	Karlheinz Scherler	André Gogoll
Guiding Idea	Ordering of structural features for lesson planning	Sensitization for acute teaching processes	Reflection of teaching processes to improve practice	Output-oriented planning and implementation of lessons
Model Concept	Prerequisite and decision fields of teaching	Contact processes of teachers, learners, and subject matter	Present facts and norms, identify problems, recommend solutions	Subject, self, and social competencies in various dimensions and stages
Didactic Method	Condition analysis, structure analysis, effect analysis	Reflect attitudes, clarify relationships, set tasks	Evaluation of teaching mishaps	Purposeful planning, cognitive activation, intensive engagement
References to General Didactics	Learning Theoretical Didactics	Communicative Didactics	Dialectical Didactics, Communicative Didactics	Educational Theoretical Didactics, Learning Theoretical Didactics

learners in such a way that the lesson is successful. Köppe (2002) places the person of PE teachers at the center of his **sports teacher didactics,** which focuses on the reflection of everyday routines and subjective theories. A model that focuses on contact processes between "I" (teacher), "We" (learning group) and "It" (matter) is the **topic-centered interaction** according to Cohn (2000). A sports didactic interpretation is still pending. Nevertheless, concrete hints are given in the explanations to the concept (see Fig. 4.6), such as how to react to deviations in the course of the lesson based on the postulate "Disturbances have priority" (Gudjons 2003, pp. 77–102). Thus, implementation didactics explicitly aims at the **process perspective** of teaching and has a certain proximity to the model of communicative didactics. In the future, references to the discussion about the quality of teaching in sports, which also focus on the teaching process, are conceivable (Richartz and Kohake 2021).

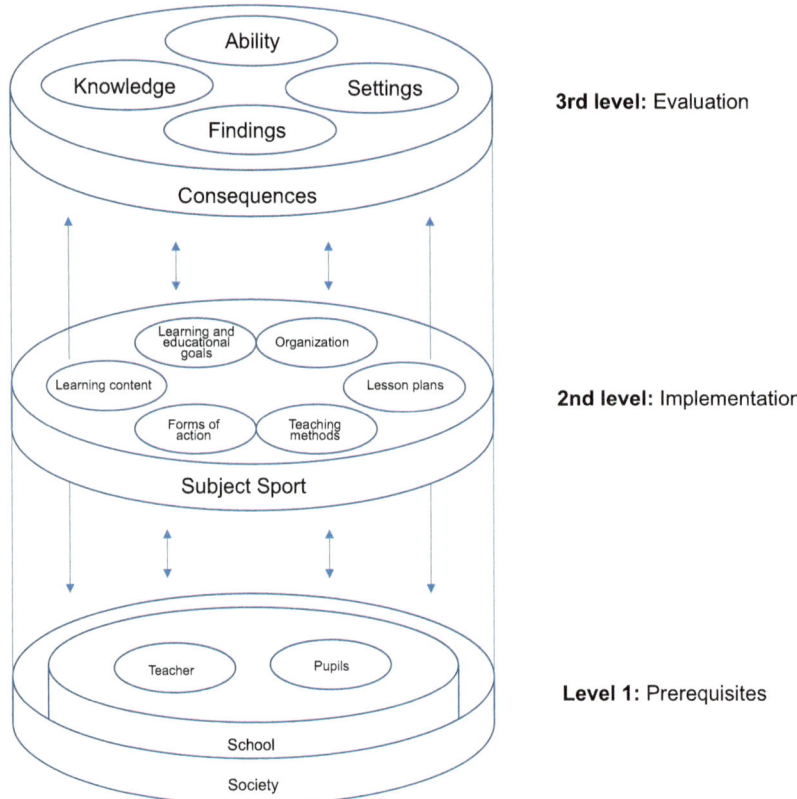

Fig. 4.5 Model of integrative-instructional sports didactics. (Mod. according to after Größing 2007, p. 37)

The model of **evaluation didactics** ("Auswertungsdidaktik") begins *after* the implementation of a sports lesson (Scherler and Schierz 1993; Scherler 2008; Wolters 2015). In contrast to planning didactics, which design plans for "good" teaching from a more or less arbitrarily set zero point, this **casuistic approach** is about reflecting on past teaching processes with the aim of improving future practice. Through the structured evaluation of cases, a **scientific case knowledge** is created, which "provides assistance through action-relieving and representative interpretations in making practical experiences reflexive when building or restructuring a skill-relevant case knowledge" (Schierz and Thiele 2002, pp. 31–32). A

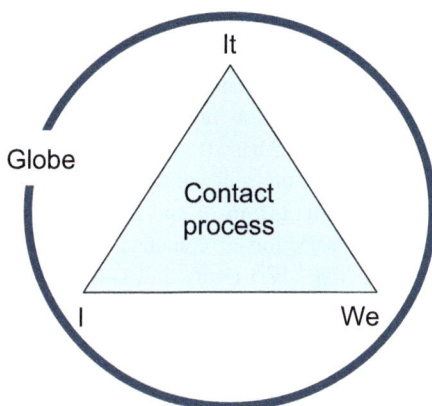

Fig. 4.6 Model of topic-centered interaction. (Mod. according to Gudjons 2003, p. 82)

basic model of casuistic sports didactics starts with the most accurate description of teaching "facts" that are related to the "norms". In the case of a "problem", there is a discrepancy between facts (being) and norms (should) of teaching, for which possible solutions are developed in a reflective processing, e.g. in sports studies. The "solutions" can consist in adapting to the facts or to the norms (see Fig. 4.7). The evaluation didactics thus also focuses on the **process perspective** of teaching and is relatede to communicative and dialectical didactics.

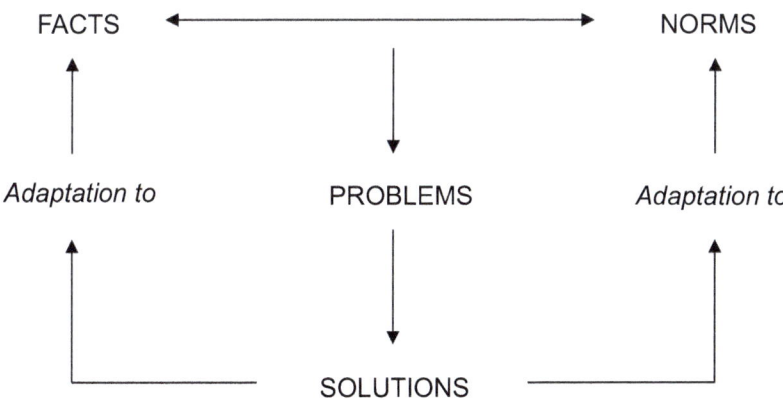

Fig. 4.7 Model of casuistic sports didactics. (Mod. according to Scherler 2008, p. 27)

The idea of a **competence-oriented didactics** ("Kompetenzorientierte Didaktik") refers back to the discussion about the standardization of (sports) teaching and the associated competence debate (Pfitzner 2021, pp. 29–32). The models presented so far essentially aim at the maturity and autonomy of the students, but are based on very different theoretical approaches (Pfitzner 2021, pp. 29–32). In the sense of a sports didactic model, the output-oriented **planning and implementation** of sports teaching is at the center, i.e. it is not primarily about the selection of content or methods, but about the result of the teaching (result perspective) (Kurz and Gogoll 2010). Depending on the approach, competences should be promoted in different dimensions and at different levels. In the approach of **sports and movement cultural competence** by Gogoll (2011), it is about access, orientation and participation competences at the pre-reflexive, factual-reflexive and intentional-reflexive level (see Fig. 4.8). In methodological terms, task setting and cognitive activation are of particular importance (cf. Pfitzner 2018). In terms of the justification of competences, there are references

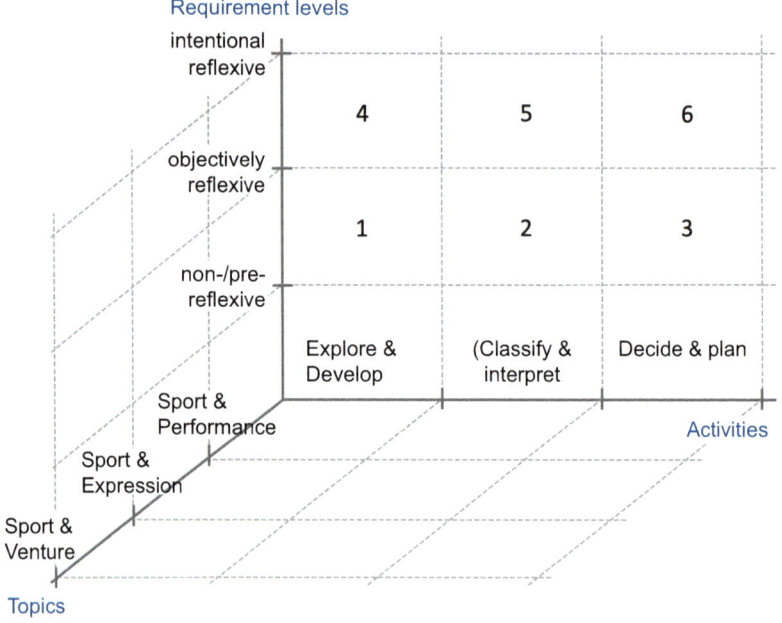

Fig. 4.8 Three-dimensional model of sports and movement cultural competence. (Mod. according to Gogoll, 2013, p. 18)

to educational-theoretical didactics. At the same time, learning-theoretical didactics offer starting points for the goal- or result-oriented planning of teaching.

▶ **Literature Tip** Pfitzner, M. (2021). Sportdidaktik. In A. Güllich & M. Krüger (Eds.), *Sport in Kultur und Gesellschaft and Society* (pp. 15–35). Berlin: Springer Spectrum.
The contribution by Michael Pfitzner provides a compact, good overview of didactic models, subject didactic concepts and empirical studies of sports didactics.

4.4   Overview of Didactic Models

Didactic models refer to the entire process of planning, implementing, and evaluating instruction, including the prerequisite and decision-making level. In contrast to didactic concepts, **didactic models** consider the prerequisites, possibilities, and consequences of instruction in a theoretically comprehensive way that also includes epistemological basic positions (see Fig. 4.9). As theoretical structures for the analysis and modeling of didactic action, their claim goes beyond the more practice-oriented claim of didactic concepts. Nevertheless, they can contribute to sharpening one's own **understanding of instruction and instructioning**. General didactic models do this in a cross-cutting, subject-independent way. **Sports didactic models**, on the other hand, include the specific subject matter and model PE instruction in a specific way. While planning didactics in sports provide an overview of the structural elements of sports instruction, evaluation didactics can help to learn from mistakes in (one's own) practice. The implementation didactics

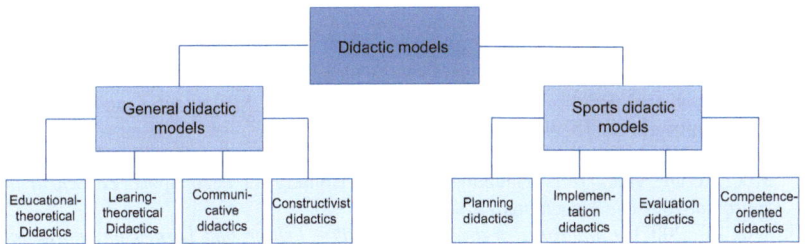

Fig. 4.9 Overview of didactic models. (Own illustration)

show the processuality of sports instruction and sensitize to the necessity of getting involved. A competence-oriented approach focuses on the output of sports instruction and can thus differentiate the objectives of the instruction.

Reflection Questions
1. What is the function of subject didactic models and concepts?
2. How do PE and PE teaching differ?
3. Why can the structural model of instruction only be used to analyze general instructional processes?
4. What is the difference between the didactic star and the didactic triangle?
5. To what extent can general didactic models usually be assigned to a certain epistemological basic position?
6. Why are didactic models not static structures?
7. What is the difference between educational-theoretical and learning -theoretical didactics?
8. To what extent do sports didactic models refer to general didactic models?
9. How do planning and evaluation didactics in sports differ?
10. What added value does implementation didactics have in sports?

References

Balz, E. (1992). Fachdidaktische Konzepte oder: Woran soll sich der Schulsport orientieren? *Sportpädagogik, 16*(2), 13–22.
Balz, E. (2021). Vier Felder des Sports – ein Modell für den Schulsport. *Sportunterricht, 70,* 57–63.
Cohn, R. (2000). *Von der Psychoanalyse zur themenzentrierten Interaktion. Von der Behandlung einzelner zu einer Pädagogik für alle* (14. edn.). Stuttgart: Klett-Cotta.
Funke-Wieneke, J. (Eds.). (1997). *Vermitteln zwischen Kind und Sache. Erläuterungen zur Sportpädagogik.* Seelze-Velber: Kallmeyer.
Gogoll, A. (2011). Auf dem Weg zu einem Kompetenzmodell für den Lernbereich „Bewegung, Spiel und Sport". In G. Stibbe (Eds.), *Standards, Kompetenzen und Lehrpläne* (Reihe Sport, 16, S. 18–30). Schorndorf: Hofmann.
Gogoll, A. (2013). Sport- und bewegungskulturelle Kompetenz – Zur Begründung und Modellierung eines Teils handlungsbezogener Bildung im Fach Sport. *Zeitschrift für sportpädagogische Forschung, 1*(2), 5–24.
Größing, S. (2007). *Einführung in die Sportdidaktik – Lehren und Lernen im Sportunterricht* (9., überarbeitete und erweiterte Aufl.). Wiebelsheim: Limpert.
Gudjons, H. (2003). Lebendig lehren und lernen – Die Themenzentrierte Interaktion (TZI) als Weg zum ganzheitlichen Unterricht. In H. Gudjons (Eds.), *Didaktik zum Anfas-*

sen – *Lehrer/in-Persönlichkeit und lebendiger Unterricht* (S. 77–102). Bad Heilbrunn: Klinkhardt.

Hänsel, F., Baumgärtner, S. D., Kornmann, J. M., & Ennigkeit, F. (2022). *Sportpsychologie*. Berlin, Heidelberg: Springer.

Haug, A. (2019). Schule als Sozialisationsinstanz. In G. Bovet & V. Huwendiek (Eds.), *Leitfaden Schulpraxis – Pädagogik und Psychologie für den Lehrberuf* (11. edn., S. 553-572). Berlin: Cornelsen.

Heimann, P., Otto, G., & Schulz, W. (1965). *Unterricht – Analyse und Planung*. Hannover: Schroedel.

Helsper, W., & Keuffer, J. (2010). Unterricht. In H.-H. Krüger & W. Helsper (Eds.), *Einführung in die Grundbegriffe und Grundfragen der Erziehungswissenschaft* (9. überarbeitete und aktualisierte Aufl., pp. 91–102). Wiesbaden: VS.

Heymen, N., & Leue, W. (2014). *Planung von Sportunterricht* (8., unveränderte Aufl.). Hohengehren: Schneider.

Huwendiek, V. (2019). Didaktische Modelle. In G. Bovet & V. Huwendiek (Eds.), *Leitfaden Schulpraxis – Pädagogik und Psychologie für den Lehrberuf* (11. edn., pp. 33–68). Berlin: Cornelsen.

Jank, W., & Meyer, H. (2020). *Didaktische Modelle* (14. edn.). Berlin: Cornelsen.

Klafki, W. (1957). *Das pädagogische Problem des Elementaren und die Theorie der kategorialen Bildung*. Weinheim: Beltz.

Klafki, W. (1995). „Schlüsselprobleme" als thematische Dimension eines zukunftsorientierten Konzepts von „Allgemeinbildung". In W. Münzinger & W. Klafki (Eds.), Schlüsselprobleme im Unterricht. *Die Deutsche Schule, 3* (Beiheft), 9–14.

Köppe, G. (2002). *Eine kleine (andere) Sportdidaktik aus Sportlehrersicht*. Hohengehren: Schneider.

Krieger, C. (2011). *Sportunterricht als Erziehungsgeschehen – zur Rekonstruktion sportunterrichtlicher Situationen aus Schüler- und Lehrersicht*. Köln: Strauß.

Krüger, M. (2020). *Einführung in die Geschichte der Leibeserziehung und des Sports – Teil 1: Von den Anfängen bis ins 18. Jahrhundert* (2., neu bearbeitete und aktualisierte Aufl.). Schorndorf: Hofmann.

Kurz, D., & Gogoll, A. (2010). Standards und Kompetenzen. In N. Fessler, A. Hummel & G. Stibbe (Eds.), *Handbuch Schulsport* (S. 227–244). Schorndorf: Hofmann.

Laging, R. (2000). Methoden im Sportunterricht. *Sportpädagogik, 24*(5), 2–9.

Messmer, R. (2013). *Fachdidaktik Sport*. Bern: Haupt UTB.

Neuber, N. (2004). Vom Wissen zum Können – oder: Brauchen wir eine „Durchführungsdidaktik"? In M. Schierz & P. Frei (Eds.), *Sportpädagogisches Wissen – Spezifik – Transfer – Transformation* (Schriften der Deutschen Vereinigung für Sportwissenschaft, 141, pp. 178–184). Hamburg: Czwalina.

Neuber, N. (2020). *Fachdidaktische Konzepte Sport – Zielgruppen und Voraussetzungen* (Basiswissen Lernen im Sport). Wiesbaden: Springer VS. https://doi.org/10.1007/978-3-658-28464-0

Neuber, N. (2021). Fachdidaktische Konzepte Sport II – Themenfelder und Perspektiven (Basiswissen Lernen im Sport). Wiesbaden: Springer VS. https://doi.org/10.1007/978-3-658-30249-8

Pfitzner, M. (2018). *Lernaufgaben im kompetenzförderlichen Sportunterricht. Theoretische Grundlagen und empirische Befunde*. Springer VS.

Pfitzner, M. (2021). Sportdidaktik. In A. Güllich & M. Krüger (Eds.), *Sport in Kultur und Gesellschaft.* (pp. 15–35). Berlin: Springer Spektrum.

Pfitzner, M., & Pürgstaller, E. (2022). Lehren, Lernen und Unterrichten im Sport – Sportdidaktik. In A. Güllich & M. Krüger (Eds.), *Sport – Das Lehrbuch für das Sportstudium* (pp. 529–561). Berlin: Springer Spektrum. https://doi.org/10.1007/978-3-662-64695-3_14

Popp, W. (Eds.). (1976). *Kommunikative Didaktik.* Weinheim: Beltz.

Prohl, R. (2010). *Grundriss der Sportpädagogik* (3. edn.). Wiebelsheim: Limpert.

Prohl, R. (2022). Der Doppelauftrag des Erziehenden Sportunterrichts. In V. Scheid & R. Prohl (Eds.), *Sportdidaktik – Grundlagen, Vermittlungsformen, Bewegungsfelder* (3., durchgesehene und korrigierte Aufl., pp. 64–84). Wiebelsheim: Limpert.

Reich, K. (1997). *Systemisch-konstruktivistische Pädagogik – Einführung in die Grundlagen einer interaktionistisch-konstruktivistischen Pädagogik* (2., durchgesehene Aufl.). Neuwied: Luchterhand.

Richartz, A., & Kohake, K. (2021). Zur (Fach-)Spezifität von Unterrichtsqualität im Fach Sport. *Unterrichtswissenschaft, 49,* 243–251.

Scherler, K. (2008). *Sportunterricht auswerten – Eine Unterrichtslehre* (2., überarbeitete Aufl.). Hamburg: Czwalina.

Scherler, K., & Schierz, M. (1993). *Sport unterrichten.* Schorndorf: Hofmann.

Schierz, M., & Thiele, J. (2002). Hermeneutische Kompetenz durch Fallarbeit. Überlegungen zum Stellenwert kasuistischer Forschung und Lehre an Beispielen antinomischen Handelns in sportpädagogischen Berufsfeldern. *Zeitschrift für Pädagogik, 48*(1), 30–47.

Söll, W. (1996). *Sportunterricht – Sport unterrichten. Ein Handbuch für Sportlehrer.* Schorndorf: Hofmann.

Terhart, E. (2019). *Didaktik – Eine Einführung.* Stuttgart: Reclam.

Terhart, E. (2021). *Didaktische Theorien und Modelle.* Hagen: Fernuniversität.

Thiele, J., & Schierz, M. (2011). Handlungsfähigkeit – revisited. Plädoyer zur Wiederaufnahme einer didaktischen Leitidee. *Spectrum der Sportwissenschaft, 23*(1), 52–75.

Treutlein, G. (1998). Veränderung der Bedeutung und Gestaltung der Beziehungsebene – Grundlage für einen zeitgemäßen Sportunterricht. *Sportunterricht, 47,* 436–443.

Weineck, J. (2019). *Optimales Training – Leistungsphysiologische Trainingslehre unter besonderer Berücksichtigung des Kinder- und Jugendtrainings* (17. edn.). Balingen: Spitta.

Wolters, P. (2015). *Fallarbeit in der Sportlehrerausbildung.* Aachen: Meyer & Meyer.

Wolters, P., Ehni, H., Kretschmer, J., Scherler, K., & Weichert, W. (2000). *Didaktik des Schulsports.* Schorndorf: Hofmann.

Didactic Concepts

5

Abstract

This chapter deals with didactic concepts for physical education. Starting from considerations on the scope and systematization of sports didactic concepts, four object-oriented concepts are presented with the types of sports concept, the concept of capacity to act in sports, the concept of basic physical and sporting education, and the concept of depedagogization of school sports. Four subject-oriented concepts are contrasted with them: the body experience concept, the psychomotor concept, the concept of aesthetic education, and the socio-ecological concept. Finally, the concepts are brought together in the sense of an integrative approach. A digression on capactiy to act in sports complements the chapter.

5.1   Introduction

General and subject-specific **models and concepts** are intended to provide basic orientations for the theoretical and practical examination of teaching-learning processes in sports. At its core, it is about understanding teaching in general and sports teaching in particular. All sports didactic approaches share the conviction that movement, game, and sports offers for children and adolescents can be pedagogically staged. In accordance with the subject culture, the considerations primarily relate to **sports in school** (Neuber 2020, p. 137–158). After German and mathematics, sports is the third largest subject taught. School sports have both intra-school and extra-school tasks. In the sense of the educational sports teaching, these tasks can be justified as subject-immanent *(education for sports)* and cross-curricular goals *(education through sports)* (Prohl 2022). In this context, education and formation   can be highlighted as central tasks of pedagogical action within the framework of **educational sports teaching** (see Sect. 3.3.3).

Physical education takes place under complex conditions. The paradoxical tension of the three **functions of school** (Haug 2019) – qualification, selection, and integration – is extended by at least one level in physical education. In addition to the basic contradiction between qualification and selection, there is the contradiction between "sports as subjective fulfillment of meaning", as many children and adolescents appreciate outside of school, and sports as a "mandatory school event", which is subject to school curricula and obligations. Prohl (2010, p. 100) calls this the **double paradox of physical education** (see Fig. 5.1). Pedagogical tasks and school conditions require that (prospective) PE teachers orient themselves and become aware of their own position in order to be able to act justifiably. Sports didactics offer sports didactic **models and concepts** for this, which are presented in this and the previous chapter. Introduction and basic terms are the same in both chapters (see Chap. 4). *Specific* subject-specific concepts of *medium* range are presented elsewhere (Neuber 2020, 2021).

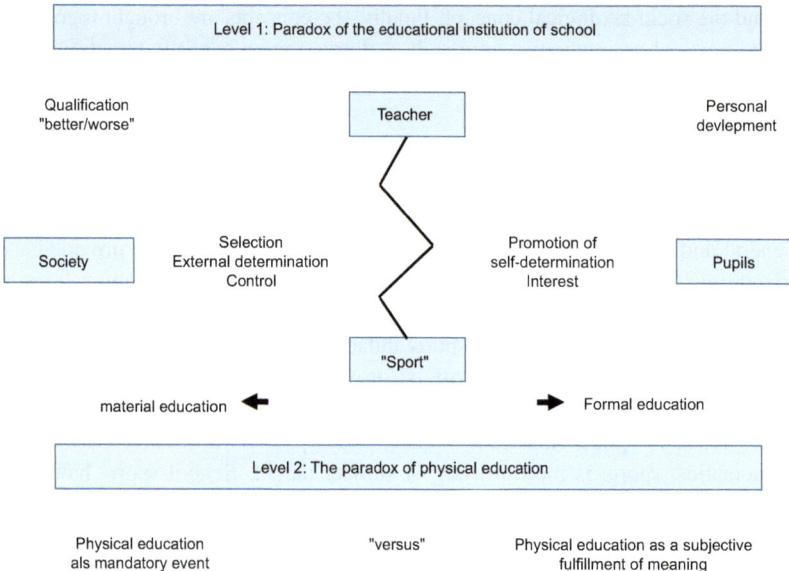

Fig. 5.1   Double paradox of physical education. (Mod. according to Prohl 2010, p. 100)

5.2 Basic Concepts

The basic concepts of didactic models and concepts initially include "instruction" and "instructioning".

▶ **Instruction** is the targeted planning, implementation, and evaluation of teaching-learning processes in an institutional context.

Instructioning is the activity of professional teachers, which is "more strongly bound to the mediation of content than education, help or even advice, which the teacher masters and should convey in such a way that it can be learned by learners who do not yet understand it" (Helsper and Keuffer 2010, p. 92). The **didactics** is the science of teaching and instruction (cf. Huwendiek 2019). These considerations can be applied to the subject of pyhsical education.

▶ **Physical education** is then the targeted planning, implementation, and evaluation of teaching-learning processes in the field of movement, games, and sports in an institutional context.

Teaching pyhsical education is the professional pedagogical activity of PE teachers, which aims at initiating teaching-learning processes in the field of movement, games, and sport. **Sports didactics** is the science of physical education and teaching pyhsical education. While "pyhsical education" focuses more on the structures of the teaching-learning activity, "teaching physical education" refers to the process of implementation (Scherler 2008, pp. 13–17).

The basic structures of instructional action are summarized in didactic models and concepts. A conceptual starting point is the **didactic triangle,** which describes the mutual relationships between "teacher", "student", and "subject matter" (Huwendiek 2019, p. 34). **Didactic models** are more complex. They can be understood as general "theoretical structures for analysing and modeling of didactic action in school and non-school contexts" (Jank and Meyer 2020, p. 35) (see Chap. 4). In comparison, **didactic concepts** are more implementation-oriented and denote "overall orientations of didactic-methodical action, in which a justified connection of goal, content, and method decisions is established" (Jank and Meyer 2020, p. 305). They define basic principles of teaching and usually also provide specific instructions for designing the instruction. The specific interactions of goals, contents, and methods of teaching are referred to as **implication context** (Jank and Meyer 2020, p. 55).

5.3   Foundations

The distinction between didactic models and concepts is of a gradual nature. While didactic models provide a general, rather basic orientation with regard to teaching, didactic concepts or also **teaching concepts** are more oriented towards practical instruction. They provide a "hands-on didactics" (Jank and Meyer 2020, p. 306). In this respect, they "often have a methodological accent in teaching, but they also make decisive statements about meaningful and meaningless content, about important and secondary objectives, about 'correct' and 'wrong' teacher behavior" (Jank and Meyer 2020, p. 305). On a general level, there are a variety of **didactic concepts,** such as project teaching, action-oriented teaching, open teaching, experience-oriented teaching, student-oriented teaching, genetic teaching and learning, or curriculum didactics (Jank and Meyer 2020, pp. 304–314). In addition, there are elements of the so-called **new learning culture,** such as the individualization of learning processes, the acquisition of intelligent and applied knowledge, or the role of digital media (Terhart 2019, pp. 61–65).

While general didactic concepts look at teaching at a higher level, **subject didactic concepts** focus on a specific practical teaching action field, usually a subject, e.g., physical education. They thus serve the "regionalization of education" (Jank and Meyer 2020, p. 38). Extracurricular learning fields are in principle also relevant, but so far have been less comprehensively processed than school learning fields. Subject didactic concepts in sports "are theoretical designs by sports didacticians"—as Eckart Balz (1992, p. 13) once minimally defined it. He defines the term more extensively elsewhere:

▶ **Sports didactic concepts** are "designs for a pedagogical structuring of school sports [...]; they answer questions about the mission of school sports, its guiding objectives, content, and methods" (Balz 2013, p. 34). They mark distinguishable positions that can be taken with regard to the design of school sports.

There are a variety of didactic concepts for sports with different orientations and scopes (see Fig. 5.2). Sports didactic **concepts with a small range** serve as practical teaching concepts with action-guiding ideas for PE teachers, subject conferences, and schools (cf. Regner 2005). Sports didactic **concepts with a medium range** go beyond the level of the individual school, but only focus on sub-areas of didactic action in sports, such as working with specific target groups, e.g., children and adolescents, or the promotion of certain perspectives, e.g., expression and design or performance and success. These concepts are presented in detail

Concepts with a small range

(e.g. the physical education concept for the trial level
or the school sports concept of an individual school)

Concepts with medium range

(e.g. for the target group "Children" or for the perspective
"Experience, understand and assess performance")

Concepts with a wide range

(e.g. types of sport concept or body experience concept)

Fig. 5.2   Different scopes of subject-didactic concepts in sports. (Own illustration)

elsewhere (Neuber 2000, 2021). At the content level, **didactics of sports types** or movement fields are also distinguished, such as sports game didactics or the didactics of gymnastics/dance (Pfitzner and Pürgstaller 2022, pp. 537–540). Sports didactic **concepts with a large range**, on the other hand, refer to the entire sports education and thus give "a certain planning-didactic orientation to school sports practice and curriculum development, to sports teachers—for their self-understanding and their training—as well as to the subject didactics itself" (Balz 2013, p. 34). Overviews of sports didactics usually refer to subject-didactic concepts with this comprehensive claim (e.g., Balz 2013; Pfitzner 2021; Prohl 2022).

In this sense, the following presents **sports didactic concepts** with a *large* range to show basic orientations of a sports didactics. The systematization based on more or less dichotomous guiding ideas has a certain tradition (e.g., Balz 1992; Neumann 2004; Elflein 2012; Balz 2013; Bräutigam 2015; Pfitzner 2021). Köppe (2003) also distinguishes two "orientations" in relation to sports didactic concepts: The **object-oriented orientation** starts with the movement practices of a society and includes traditional movement games, standardized sports, and movement trends. The **subject-oriented orientation** refers to a changed understanding of physicality and movement, which aims at "independently tracing one's own movement meanings, allowing social forms of play and movement to be found, and understanding observed movements" (Köppe 2003, p. 68). Prohl (2022) argues similarly, distinguishing a "pragmatic-qualifying current" from a "critical-emancipatory current" in relation to sports didactic concepts. While he assigns the first current to material education concepts and thus more to the matter "sports", he relates the second current to formal education concepts and thus more to the subject.

▶   **Literature Tip** Scheid, V., & Prohl, R. (Eds.). (2022). *Sportdidaktik – Grun-
        dlagen, Vermittlungsformen, Bewegungsfelder* (3rd, revised and cor-
        rected edition). Wiebelsheim: Limpert.
            In their anthology, Volker Scheid and Robert Prohl provide an over-
        view of the basics and movement fields of sports didactics. It includes
        contributions on subject-didactic currents and on educational sports
        teaching.

In addition to systematization based on certain guiding ideas, there are other approaches. Against the backdrop of postmodern theories, Schierz (1997) moves away from the "grand designs" and advocates for "small stories" in physical education in the sense of a **narrative didactics**. In doing so, he follows the tradition of evaluation didactic models (see Sect. 4.3.2). It remains to be discussed how a general orientation can emerge from the variety of individual teaching situations. Messmer (2013) also understands his "subject model sport" in an evaluation didactic way and develops a **didactics of showing,** which conceives sport as a societal practice and which should present the "diversity of sports" to the learners (Messmer 2013, p. 32). In this way, he structures his didactics not primarily along pedagogical guiding ideas, but along the "matter of sport", e.g. in the form of conditional abilities, motor, game tactical or aesthetic competencies. However, it remains to be clarified what exactly constitutes the societal practice of sports (cf. Beckers 1993). Against the backdrop of these open questions, the following selection of sports didactic concepts refers to the two tasks of pedagogical action in sports (see chapter 1) and adopts the terminology of Köppe (2003). In this sense, selected **object- and subject-oriented concepts** are presented to sharpen one's own position. In a concluding overview, an integrative perspective is taken that combines the two understandings.

5.3.1 Object-oriented Concepts

▶ **Object-oriented concepts** in sports didactics start from the societal-cultural reality of sports and primarily aim at the exploration of movement, game, and sports culture. Thus, they are more sports(type)oriented and methodically closed-oriented (see Table 5.1).

Among the classics of object-oriented approaches is the **types of sport concept** ("Sportartenkonzept") by Wolfang Söll (1995, 2000). The basic idea is that the subject structure of traditional sports is so formative that physical education should be oriented towards it. This means that sports "are not interchangeable, they must be taught according to their own structure of the demands they make" (Söll 1995, p. 65). The guiding idea of the sports concept is therefore the **exploration of (extracurricular) sports culture,** which is expressed in traditional

Table 5.1 Overview of object-oriented didactic concepts

	Types of sport concept	Concept of capacity to act in sport	Concept of basic physical and sportingeducation	Concept of depedagogization
Representative	Wolfgang Söll	Dietrich Kurz	Albrecht Hummel	Meinhart Volkamer
Guiding idea	Exploration of sports culture	Capacity to act in sports	Motor performance and sports skills	Distinction from excessive pedagogization and instrumentalization of sports
Subject reference	Sports in the narrower sense: traditional sports	Sports in the broader sense: sports and movement trends	Physical abilities and sports	"Actual", unadulterated sports
Teaching reference	Closed-deductive	Closed-deductive; perspectives of meaning	Closed-deductive; appreciation of practicing, training, and stressing	Open-deductive; without specifications

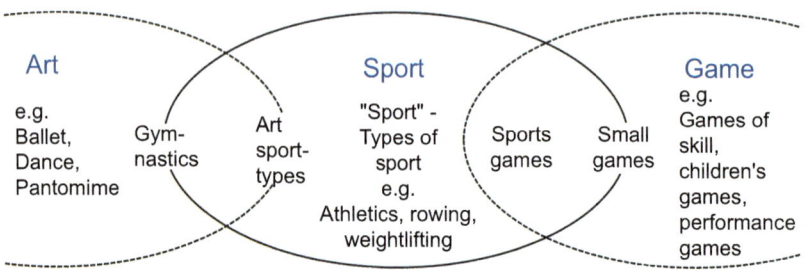

Fig. 5.3 Content areas of the sports concept. (Mod. according to Söll 2005, p. 37)

individual and team sports as well as in gymnastics/dance (see Fig. 5.3). There
is no further pedagogical interest, as "the sports are essential carriers of meaning in sports and carry the decisive didactic approaches" within themselves (Söll
1995, p. 65). Based on the subject structure of this **sports in the narrower sense,**
the teaching approach is closed-deductive; learning primarily takes place through
instruction and correction. The approach continues to shape many practical offerings in sports clubs, schools, and universities, even if it probably rarely appears in
its pure form.

The **concept of capacity to act in sports** ("Handlungsfähigkeit im Sport") by
Dietrich Kurz (1990, 1995) also starts from the subject structure of sports, but
substantially expands Söll's considerations by aiming at comprehensive action
competence in (extracurricular) sports. Based on motivational psychological
considerations, six "perspectives of meaning" are introduced with performance,
tension, togetherness, health, impression, and expression, which give direction
to the sports participants' activity. In a later interpretation, these perspectives of
meaning become **pedagogical perspectives,** which are "applied" to sports by
teachers with educational intent, thus prescribing a certain reading of sports (Kurz
2013, p. 21). This pragmatic didactics also draws on sports, but is in principle
open to extensions of the sports canon, for example in the sense of movement
trends ("sports in the broader sense"). The methodological approach is generally
closed-deductive, but offers opportunities for self-responsible action in the sense
of subjective **attributions of meaning.** After the idea of action competence was
initially considered outdated with the introduction of the dual mandate (MSWWF
NRW, 1999), it has been experiencing a certain renaissance in recent years.

Capacity to act in Sports ("Handlungsfähigkeit im Sport")
The idea of capacity to act in sports has been shaping the didactic discussion for many years. According to the theory of physical education and the sports curriculum (see Sect. 4.3.2), the concept of capacity to act was established in the 1980s as the third major **guiding idea of school sports** in Germany. The starting point of agency were two fundamental writings, both published in 1977: Horst Ehni (1977) poses in his book *Sport and School Sports* the question of the meaning of sports, which in his view arises from the actions and experiences of the students (Ehni 2000, p. 29). For him, multiperspectivity means "making the subject of sports meaningful through multiple and different actions" (Ehni 2000, p. 32). This approach assumes a sport-immanent purpose of sports. Accordingly, **capacity to act in sports** simply means "the ability to act" in sports (Ehni 2000, p. 32). Horst Ehni thus develops a didactics of showing, which is later taken up by Messmer (2013) in his subject model of sports. However, this understanding of capacity to act was not able to gain widespread acceptance.

The second approach, published in 1977, was different. The *Elements of School Sports* by Dietrich Kurz have significantly shaped the didactic discussion and also became the model for the 1980s guidelines and curricula (Aschebrock 2013). Kurz also starts from the subject of sports when he asks: "What experiences should students make in sports, what should they learn about and in it, in what way should their development be influenced by it?" (Kurz 1977, p. 9). In contrast to Ehni, he draws on empirical studies from the 1970s that describe the meaning of sports in six **perspectives of meaning**. Multiperspectivity can thus be summarized in these six meaning perspectives or pedagogical perspectives. **Capacity to act in sports** then means getting to know these motives or perspectives in the context of sports lessons and being able to apply them outside of lessons (Kurz 2013). The guiding idea of capacity to act was replaced by the idea of educational physical education at the end of the 1990s.

Nevertheless, there are efforts to strengthen capacity to act as a core concept in sports didactics. Thus, Balz and Neumann repeatedly refer to the idea of capacity to act in their work on a **pragmatic sports didactics** (e.g. Balz and Neumann 2021). Capacity to act is also the guiding idea in the integrative approach of the intermediary concept (see Sect. 5.4). In addition, Thiele and Schierz (2011) advocate a revival of the idea of capacity to act by expanding it with a perspective on inequality. They draw on the "capabilities approach" from educational science, which focuses on "the question of the conditions for leading a good or successful life for as many people as possible, ideally all people" (Thiele and Schierz 2011, p. 55). Capacity to act then means **enabling action** even under unfavorable conditions. In relation to school sports, this means: "Physical education should not be limited to mere transmission of skills and knowledge in the execution of sports content, but should be conceptually transformed to prepare opportunities for participation and judgement, which are conveyed through the pluralization of forms of experience, criticism and ways of reflection" (Thiele and Schierz 2011, p. 71). In this view, the sports didactic idea of capacity to act still offers considerable potential.

▶   **Literature Tip** Kurz, D. (1977). *Elemente des Schulsports – Grundlagen einer pragmatischen Fachdidaktik.* Schorndorf: Hofmann.
       The habilitation thesis of Dietrich Kurz is one of the classics of sports didactics. In it, he establishes his concept of capacity to act, which continues to influence the didactic discussion to this day.

The concept of **basic physical and sporting education** ("Körperlich-sportliche Grundlagenbildung") goes back to Albrecht Hummel (1997). It has its roots in the "physical basic *training*" of the pedagogy of the GDR, whose main task was the development of physical performance (Hummel 1994). After the fall of the Berlin Wall, the concept was further developed in the sense of the dual *education* of physical and sporting basics. The starting points of the approach lie in the **structural nature of the body** and the **matter of sport** (see Fig. 5.4). Accordingly, the goals are a "best possible organismic and motor performance (fitness) and a 'good' posture" as well as the "best possible development of conditional and coordinative abilities" (Hummel 2013, p. 114). This is supplemented by a contribution to the general ability to act in sport and the development of sporting skills. Methodically, the concept relies on closed-deductive stagings, which are characterized by a high **"appreciation of practicing, training and stressing"** (Hummel 2013, p. 115). Overall, there is a close proximity to the (West German) sports concept of Söll (1995), with the references to training science basics being even more pronounced. It is therefore not surprising that from a sports pedagogical perspective, there has been some severe criticism of the underlying educational concept of the approach (Beckers 2001).

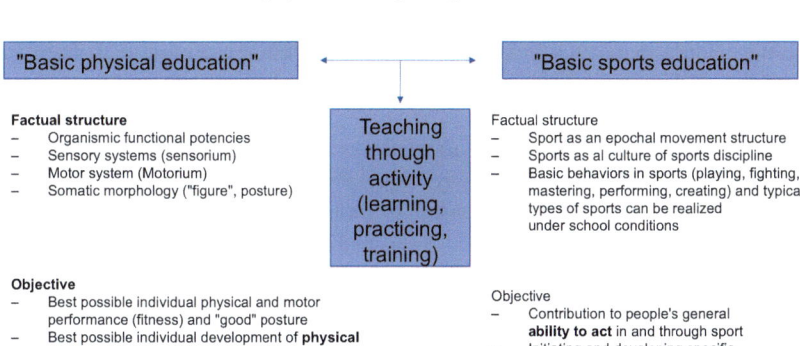

The basic artistic dimensions of basic
physical and sporting education

Fig. 5.4 Basic dimensions of physical-sporting basic education. (Mod. according to Hummel 2013, p. 114)

The concept of **depedagogization of school sports** ("Entpädagogisierung") by Meinhart Volkamer (1987) is cross to the concepts presented so far. The approach is against an excessive pedagogization of physical education. Pedagogical objectives, such as health and social education, meant an impermissible **instrumentalization of sports** (Volkamer 1987, p. 154). Accordingly, the subject matter is seen in a "return to the actual, unadulterated essence of sports. Sport is understood as voluntary, consequence-free, body-focused action" (Balz 1992, p. 16)—the sport should "just be fun". Accordingly general is the methodical concept: "A good method is then and only then meaningful, when the student wants to learn the offered movement, experiences it as meaningful" (Volkamer and Zimmer 1984, p. 229). Overall, the concept thus turns against a **pedagogical staging of sports** in school—which usually leads to students demanding the sport they know from extracurricular scenes. Thus, the approach of depedagogization is ultimately strongly object-oriented, because it focusses on the matter of (extracurricular) sports in the center.

5.3.2   Subject-oriented Concepts

▶ **Subject-oriented concepts** of sports didactics start from the individual possibilities and desires of the individual and aim at promoting the subject. They are
therefore more movement-oriented and methodically open (cf. Table 5.2)

Among the classics of subject-oriented concepts is the **body experience concept** ("Körpererfahrungskonzept") by Jürgen Funke-Wieneke (1992, 2009). It can
be understood as a counter-movement to traditional "instruction, teaching and
training methods" (Funke-Wieneke 2009, p. 319). It has often been referred to
as the counterpoint to the types of sportconcept by Söll (2000). The main idea
of the body experience concept aims at the **perception of one's own body,** also
in contrast to standardized body practices in normative competitive sports. This
does not mean that traditional sports are excluded; in fact, the concept has been
extensively related to well-known sports (Treutlein et al. 1992). However, it also
makes use of numerous body experience practices from New Games and Modern
Dance to Tai-Chi and Yoga to sauna bathing. The emancipatory concern in the

Table 5.2 Overview of subject-oriented didactic concepts

	Body experi-ence concept	Psychomotor concept	Concept of aesthetic edu-cation	Socio-ecologi-cal concept
Representative	Jürgen Funke-Wienke	Renate Zimmer	Ursula Fritsch	Knut Dietrich
Guiding idea	Perception of one's own body; questioning of sports patterns	Development promotion through perception and movement	Experience of the world through percep-tion and compo-sition	Development promotion and exploration of movement culture
Subject refer-ence	Basic themes of movement: instrumental, sensitive, social, symbolic	Movement and play	Open movement offers, play and dance	Everyday movement and play opportu-nities
Teaching refer-ence	Open-inductive; "self-educa-tion"; differen-tiation	Open-inductive; help for self-help	Partially open-inductive; resistance and foreignness as principles	Open-induc-tive; staging of conditions

sense of a **"self-education"**, which lies in breaking through traditional sports patterns and critically questioning societal (movement) practices, cannot be denied (Funke-Wieneke 2009, p. 318). So-called **basic themes of movement** can be interpreted instrumentally, sensitively, socially and symbolically (see Fig. 5.5). Methodologically, the body experience concept tends to work inductively-open, but also uses targeted differentiation (Kolb 1994). The body experience concept has often polarized in its history—however, it is undisputed that it has contributed to the further development of sports didactics (Neuber 2021, pp. 31–50).

The **psychomotor concept** ("Psychomotorisches Konzept") by Renate Zimmer (2003, 2019) assumes an interlocking of psychological and physical processes. Movement action is understood as developmental action (Fischer 2019). Essential reference points of a psychomotor development promotion are **perception and movement.** The guiding idea of psychomotricity is the development of a harmonious personality through movement and play (Zimmer 2019). This means that the matter of sports takes a back seat: "Here, it is more about the *child,* who is given the opportunity to test himself through movement, to experience his body, to recognize and develop his abilities" (Zimmer 1996, p. 75). For this purpose, psychomotricity works with both open movement landscapes and guided movement offers that rely on the self-activity of the children. In methodological terms, an open-inductive approach is pursued, which is understood in the sense of **help for self-help.** The psychomotor concept was developed especially

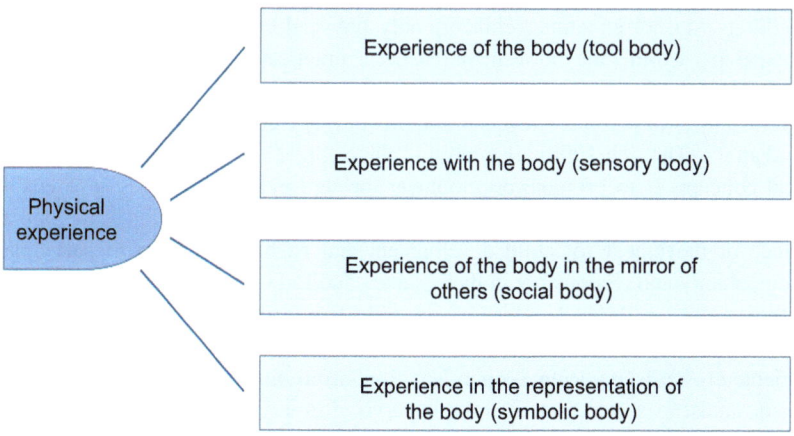

Fig. 5.5 Dimensions of corporeality/basic themes of movement. (Mod. according to Funke-Wieneke 2009, p. 318)

for children in pre-school and primary school age, but today there are psychomotor approaches for all age groups up to old age (Köckenberger 2003). However, in school sports, it is mainly used in primary education.

The concept of **aesthetic education** ("Ästhetische Erziehung") by Ursula Fritsch (2007) is based on subjective experiences in a complex world. The goal of aesthetic movement education is to make the world present, to "translate" perceptions and experiences into one's own designs. A person can express "what he has experienced, what has happened to him, what he feels and senses, through e.g. images, sounds, movements, poetic language; he can make it symbolically present to himself and others" (Fritsch 1989, p. 11). In contrast to discursive, conceptual confrontation, aesthetic-symbolic action offers the possibility to articulate even the "unspeakable". The terms **perception** and **composition** are central. In terms of content, all movement, play and sports offers can basically be used. In primary school, open movement and play forms are mainly used (Bannmüller 2000), while in secondary school, elements from gymnastics/dance are in the foreground (Fritsch 2007). Methodically, aesthetic education starts with the perception of the individually new, the "for me extraordinary and unusual, the contradictory" (Beckers 1997, p. 21). To this end, principles of **resistance and strangeness** should bring disorder into the accustomed world of perception in order to break through common patterns of perception (Klinge, 2009).

The **socio-ecological approach** (Sozial-ökologisches Konzept") starts with the change in the living environments of children and adolescents and emphasizes the design of movement-friendly spaces (Dietrich and Landau 1999). Because children "do not encounter child-friendly physical environmental conditions in their living world", the "movement teacher is practically forced […] to artificially recreate child-friendly movement opportunities" (Hildebrandt 1993, p. 269). The same applies to juvenile movement cultures (Wopp 2007). The terms **movement** and **space** (Dietrich 1998) are central to this approach. The goal of socio-ecological concepts is to promote development through movement, but also to enable participation in cultural movement life. It is about "paying attention to the importance of movement for child development and enabling children to participate competently and responsibly in their current and future movement culture" (Kretschmer 1997, p. 169). Teaching topics arise from the reference to the personal, social and material environment. Methodically, socio-ecological approaches are oriented towards **experience-open learning situations,** e.g. in the form of movement landscapes, which need to be supervised in a differentiated manner. In the 1990s, socio-ecological approaches experienced a heyday. In times of all-day schools, the topic of space is gaining greater importance today (Derecik 2018).

5.4   Overview of didactic Concepts

Subject-didactic concepts refer to the overall process of planning, implementing and evaluating teaching, including the prerequisite and decision level. In contrast to didactic models, subject-didactic concepts focus on the practical field of teaching, whereby they can refer to a single school *(small range)*, a specific topic *(medium range)* or physical education as a whole *(large range)*. Subject-didactic **concepts of large range** provide concrete suggestions for teaching ideas, understanding of the subject matter and methodology, based on the respective interpretation of the school sports mission. In reference to the two tasks of pedagogical action in sports (see Chap. 1), they can be divided into object-oriented and subject-oriented concepts. In the first case, the mediation of the matter "sport" is in the foreground *(material education concept)*, in the second case the development of the individual *(formal education concept)*.

Following this logic of systematization, didactic concepts, such as the types fo sportconcept (Söll 2005), the concept of capactiy to act in sports (Kurz 1995), the concept of basic physical and sporting education (Hummel 1997) and the concept of depedagogization of school sports (Volkamer 1987), can be assigned to the **object-oriented concepts**. These are concepts that "take the term *sports education* literally and derive the didactic justification of the subject mainly from the societal phenomenon of sports and its structural nature" (Prohl 2022, p. 53). These concepts argue predominantly sports-oriented and are methodologically rather closed. Didactic concepts, such as the concept of body experience (Funke-Wieneke 2009), the concept of psychomotor skills (Zimmer 2019), aesthetic movement education (Fritsch 2007) or the socio-ecological approach (Dietrich and Landau 1999), can be assigned to the **subject-oriented concepts**. These approaches rather focus on the subject and the pedagogical legitimation of sports, which means that "sports are critically questioned regarding their educational potentials" (Prohl 2022, p. 54). Accordingly, these concepts are rather movement-oriented and methodologically open (see Fig. 5.6).

In school practice, both object- and subject-oriented approaches are likely to be equally relevant. Therefore, it seems obvious to combine the two trends in an integrative concept. Eckart Balz (2013) has proposed the **intermediary concept** ("Intermediäres Konzept") for this purpose (see Tab. 5.3). In it, he contrasts a "conservative concept" that aims at sports motor skills with an "alternative" concept that is directed at the development of movement identity. The connecting "intermediary concept" focusses on the leading idea of capacity to act in sports. This idea "does not merely occupy a 'middle position', it does not represent a

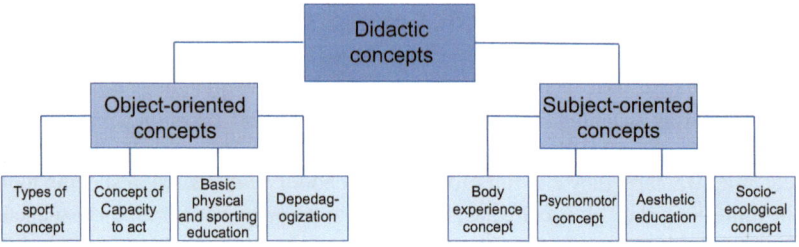

Fig. 5.6   Overview of sports didactic concepts. (Own illustration)

Tab. 5.3   Intermediary concept as a connecting concept. (Mod. according to Balz 2013, p. 38)

Concept Characteristics	Conservative Concept	Intermediary Concept	Alternative concept
Basic alignment	"Specialist didactics of reduced demands"	Pragmatic Subject didactics	Emancipatory subject didactics
Central idea	Sporting ability	Capacity to act	Movement ability
Educational figure	Material education	Categorical education	Formal education
Educational claim	Education for sport	Education in sport	Education through movement
Target level	Motor skills and abilities	Pedagogical Perspectives	Movement experiences/ movement development
Content level	Types of sport	Sport in the broader sense	Movement
Method level	Teacher-centered	(multi-)perspective	Open
Function	affirmative	complementary	corrective
Teaching example	Series of exercises for the handspring overhandspring	Lesson plans for the Taking the risk "Rollover"	Movement project for rollover experience

compromise or a mixture, but it is—as the word 'intermediary' says—an independent concept in between, capable of *bridging* supposed contradictions between sports and the individual" (Balz 2013, p. 37). Ultimately, Balz combines material and formal educational concepts in the sense of a **categorical education** (see Sect. 4.3.1) and links "education to sports" and "education through sports" in the sense of "education in sports" (Balz 2013, p. 38).

The intermediary concept shows clear parallels to the concept of an **Educational Physical Education**. In this respect, it indeed represents a bridge between sports- and movement-oriented concepts. However, it remains to be discussed to what extent an explicitly pragmatic approach can meet the formulated education-al-theoretical claim (cf. Beckers 2001). Beyond conceptual discussions, it seems sensible to combine object- and subject-oriented approaches in the sense of an education for sports and through sports (see Sect. 3.3.3). Both standardized sports and subjectively significant occasions of movement are taken into account. At the same time, the entire spectrum of closed to open teaching methods can be used (see Sect. 6.4). Similarly comprehensive is the concept of **Individual Promotion**, which was developed within the framework of general educational science considerations. Its transfer to physical education is therefore particularly capable of connecting to the school pedagogical argumentation (see Chap. 7).

Reflection Questions

1. What is function of subject-didactic models and concepts?
2. How do physical education and teaching physical education differ?
3. To what extent do sports didactic concepts with different ranges pursue different objectives?
4. What do the systematizations of sports didactic concepts usually orient themselves on?
5. To what extent does the intermediary concept form a bridge between object- and subject-oriented concepts?
6. Why do object-oriented concepts usually follow a deductive-closed methodological approach?
7. How do the sports concept and the concept of action competence in sports differ?
8. Why do subject-oriented concepts focus mor on human movement than towards standardized sports?
9. How do the body experience concept and the concept of aesthetic education differ?
10. To what extent is the concept of Educational Physical Education an integrative sports didactic concept?

References

Aschebrock, H. (2013). Vom Sportartenprogramm zur Kompetenzorientierung – zum Wandel curricularer Leitideen. In H. Aschebrock & G. Stibbe (Eds.), *Didaktische Konzepte für den Schulsport* (pp. 53–78). Aachen: Meyer & Meyer.

Balz, E. (1992). Fachdidaktische Konzepte oder: Woran soll sich der Schulsport orientieren? *Sportpädagogik, 16*(2), 13–22.

Balz, E. (2013). Fachdidaktische Konzepte. In P. Neumann, & E. Balz (Eds.), *Sportdidaktik – Pragmatische Fachdidaktik für die Sekundarstufe I und II* (pp. 34–42). Berlin: Cornelsen.

Balz, E., & Neumann, P. (2021). *Mehrperspektivischer Sportunterricht – Evaluation und Innovation.* Schorndorf: Hofmann.

Bannmüller, E. (2000). Der Zusammenhang von Wahrnehmung und Bewegung – Eine Grundlage für eine elementare Bewegungserziehung in der Grundschule. In G. Köppe & P. Elflein (Eds.), *Didaktische Perspektivenvielfalt bei Bewegung, Spiel und Sport in der Grundschule* (pp. 15–22). Hamburg: Czwalina.

Beckers, E. (1993). Der Instrumentalisierungs-Vorwurf: Ende des Nachdenkens oder Alibi für die eigene Position? *Sportwissenschaft, 23,* 233–258.

Beckers, E. (1997). Über das Bildungspotential des Sportunterrichts. In E. Balz & P. Neumann (Eds.), *Wie pädagogisch soll der Schulsport sein?* (pp. 15–32). Schorndorf: Hofmann.

Beckers, E. (2001). Renaissance des Bildungsbegriffs in der Sportpädagogik? – Orientierungssuche zwischen Widerstand und Aushöhlung. In R. Prohl (Eds.), *Bildung und Bewegung* (Schriften der Deutschen Vereinigung für Sportwissenschaft, 120, pp. 29–42). Hamburg: Czwalina.

Bräutigam, M. (2015). *Sportdidaktik – Ein Lehrbuch in 12 Lektionen* (5. edn.). Aachen: Meyer & Meyer.

Derecik, A. (2018). Übergeordnete Prinzipien zur Gestaltung von Freiräumen auf Schulhöfen und im Schulgelände. In K. Althoff & U. Gebken (Eds.), *Bewegung, Spiel und Sport für alle* (pp. 106–113). Hildesheim: Arete.

Dietrich, K. (1998). Spielräume zum Aufwachsen. *Sportpädagogik, 22*(6), 14–25.

Dietrich, K., & Landau, G. (1999). *Sportpädagogik – Grundlagen, Positionen, Tendenzen.* Butzbach-Griedel: Afra.

Ehni, H. (1977). *Sport und Schulsport – Didaktische Analysen und Beispiele aus der schulischen Praxis.* Schorndorf: Hofmann.

Ehni, H. (2000). Vom Sinn des Schulsports. In P. Wolters, H. Ehni, J. Kretschmer, K. Scherler & W. Weichert (Eds.), *Didaktik des Schulsports* (pp. 9–35). Schorndorf: Hofmann.

Elflein, P. (2012). *Sportpädagogik und Sportdidaktik* (4. edn.). Baltmannsweiler: Schneider.

Fischer, K. (2019). *Einführung in die Psychomotorik* (4., überarbeitete und erweiterte Aufl.). München: Reinhardt.

Fritsch, U. (1989). Ästhetische Erziehung: Der Körper als Ausdrucksorgan. *Sportpädagogik, 14*(5), 11 16.

Fritsch, U. (2007). Ästhetische Erziehung. In R. Laging (Eds.), *Neues Taschenbuch des Sportunterrichts. Kompaktausgabe* (3., veränderte und korrigierte Aufl., pp. 36–46). Hohengehren: Schneider.

Funke-Wieneke, J. (1992). Die Perspektive der Körpererfahrung und ihre Bedeutung bei der gezielten Vermittlung im Turnen. In G. Treutlein, J. Funke & N. Sperle (Eds.), *Körpererfahrung im Sport. Wahrnehmen – lernen – Gesundheit fördern* (2., überarbeitete Aufl.) (pp. 131–139). Aachen: Meyer & Meyer.

Funke-Wieneke, J. (2009). Körpererfahrung. In H. Haag, & A. Hummel (Eds.), *Handbuch Sportpädagogik* (2., erweiterte Aufl., pp. 314–322). Schorndorf: Hofmann.

Haug, A. (2019). Schule als Sozialisationsinstanz. In G. Bovet & V. Huwendiek (Eds.), *Leitfaden Schulpraxis – Pädagogik und Psychologie für den Lehrberuf* (11. edn., pp. 555 574). Berlin: Cornelsen.

Helsper, W., & Keuffer, J. (2010). Unterricht. In H.-H. Krüger & W. Helsper (Eds.), *Einführung in die Grundbegriffe und Grundfragen der Erziehungswissenschaft* (9. überarbeitete und aktualisierte Aufl., pp. 91–102). Wiesbaden: VS.

Hildebrandt, R. (1993). Lebensweltbezug – Leitmotiv für eine Neuorientierung der Bewegungserziehung in der Grundschule. *Sportwissenschaft, 23,* 259–275.

Hummel, A. (1994). Die Konzeption der körperlich-sportlichen Grundlagenbildung – Weiterhin eine tragfähige Leitidee. In M. Schierz, A. Hummel & E. Balz (Eds.), *Sportpädagogik: Orientierungen – Leitideen – Konzepte* (Schriften der Deutschen Vereinigung für Sportwissenschaft, 58, pp. 133–153). St. Augustin: Academia.

Hummel, A. (1997). Die körperlich-sportliche Grundlagenbildung – immer noch aktuell. In E. Balz & P. Neumann (Eds.), *Wie pädagogisch soll der Schulsport sein?* (pp. 47–62). Schorndorf: Hofmann.

Hummel, A. (2013). Körperlich-sportliche Grundlagenbildung – eine zeitgemäße Alternative. In H. Aschebrock & G. Stibbe (Eds.), *Didaktische Konzepte für den Schulsport* (pp. 99–121). Aachen: Meyer & Meyer.

Huwendiek, V. (2019). Didaktische Modelle. In G. Bovet & V. Huwendiek (Eds.), *Leitfaden Schulpraxis – Pädagogik und Psychologie für den Lehrberuf* (11. edn., pp. 33–68). Berlin: Cornelsen.

Jank, W., & Meyer, H. (2020). *Didaktische Modelle* (13. edn.). Berlin: Cornelsen Scriptor.

Klinge, A. (2009). Körperwahrnehmung: den Körper wahrnehmen, mit dem Körper wahrnehmen und verstehen. In R. Laging (Eds.), *Inhalte und Themen des Sportunterrichts* (pp. 96–107). Hohengehren: Schneider.

Köckenberger, H. (Eds.). (2003). *Psychomotorik – Ansätze und Arbeitsfelder.* Dortmund: Modernes Lernen.

Kolb, M. (1994). Methodische Prinzipien zur Entwicklung der Körperwahrnehmung. In M. Schierz, A. Hummel & E. Balz (Eds.), *Sportpädagogik. Orientierungen, Leitideen, Konzepte* (Schriften der Deutschen Vereinigung für Sportwissenschaft, 58, pp. 239–260). St. Augustin: Academia.

Köppe, G. (2003). Zur Vielfalt sportdidaktischer Perspektiven oder: Woran soll sich der Schulsport in der Grundschule orientieren? In G. Köppe & J. Schwier (Eds.), *Handbuch Grundschulsport* (pp. 63–75). Hohengehren: Schneider.

Kretschmer, J. (1997). Akzente kindgerechter Bewegungserziehung. In E. Balz & P. Neumann (Eds.), *Wie pädagogisch soll der Schulsport sein?* (pp. 169–184). Schorndorf: Hofmann.

Kurz, D. (1977). *Elemente des Schulsports – Grundlagen einer pragmatischen Fachdidaktik.* Schorndorf: Hofmann.

Kurz, D. (1990). *Elemente des Schulsports* (3. edn.). Schorndorf: Hofmann.

Kurz, D. (1995). Handlungsfähigkeit im Sport – Leitidee eines mehrperspektivischen Unterrichtskonzepts. In A. Zeuner, G. Senf, & S. Hofmann (Eds.), *Sport unterrichten – Anspruch und Wirklichkeit* (pp. 41–48). St. Augustin: Academia.

Kurz, D. (2013). Zur Entwicklung einer pragmatischen Fachdidaktik. In P. Neumann, & E. Balz (Eds.), *Sportdidaktik – Pragmatische Fachdidaktik für die Sekundarstufe I und II* (pp. 13–23). Berlin: Cornelsen.

Messmer, R. (2013). *Fachdidaktik Sport.* Bern: Haupt UTB.

MSWWF NRW (Ministerium für Schule und Weiterbildung, Wissenschaft und Forschung des Landes Nordrhein-Westfalen). (1999). *Richtlinien und Lehrpläne für die Sekundarstufe II – Gymnasium/Gesamtschule in Nordrhein-Westfalen. Sport.* Frechen: Ritterbach.

Neuber, N. (2020). *Fachdidaktische Konzepte Sport – Zielgruppen und Voraussetzungen* (Basiswissen Lernen im Sport). Wiesbaden: Springer VS. https://doi.org/10.1007/978-3-658-28464-0.

Neuber, N. (2021). *Fachdidaktische Konzepte Sport II – Themenfelder und Perspektiven* (Basiswissen Lernen im Sport). Wiesbaden: Springer VS. https://doi.org/10.1007/978-3-658-30249-8.

Neumann, P. (2004). *Erziehender Sportunterricht – Grundlagen und Perspektiven.* Baltmannsweiler: Schneider.

Pfitzner, M. (2021). Sportdidaktik. In A. Güllich, & M. Krüger (Eds.), *Sport in Kultur und Gesellschaft.* https://doi.org/10.1007/978-3-662-53385-7_22-1.

Pfitzner, M., & Pürgstaller, E. (2022). Lehren, Lernen und Unterrichten im Sport – Sportdidaktik. In A. Güllich & M. Krüger (Eds.), *Sport – Das Lehrbuch für das Sportstudium* (pp. 529–561). Berlin: Springer Spektrum. https://doi.org/10.1007/978-3-662-64695-3_14.

Prohl, R. (2010). *Grundriss der Sportpädagogik* (3. edn.). Wiebelsheim: Limpert.

Prohl, R. (2022). Sportdidaktische Orientierungen. In V. Scheid & R. Prohl (Eds.), *Sportdidaktik – Grundlagen, Vermittlungsformen, Bewegungsfelder* (3., durchgesehene und korrigierte Aufl., pp. 49–63). Wiebelsheim: Limpert.

Regner, J. (2005). *Schuleigene Lehrpläne im Sport – Grundlagen, Erfahrungen, Perspektiven.* Berlin: Pro Business.

Scheid, V., & Prohl, R. (Eds.). (2022). *Sportdidaktik – Grundlagen, Vermittlungsformen, Bewegungsfelder* (3., durchgesehene und korrigierte Aufl.). Wiebelsheim: Limpert.

Scherler, K. (2008). *Sportunterricht auswerten – Eine Unterrichtslehre* (2., überarbeitete Aufl.). Hamburg: Czwalina.

Schierz, M. (1997). *Narrative Didaktik – von den großen Entwürfen zu den kleinen Geschichten im Sportunterricht.* Weinheim, Basel: Beltz.

Söll, W. (1995). Sportunterricht ohne Sportarten? Plädoyer für ein richtig verstandenes „Sportartenkonzept". In A. Zeuner, G. Senf & S. Hofmann (Eds.), *Sport unterrichten – Anspruch und Wirklichkeit* (pp. 64–71). St. Augustin: Academia.

Söll, W. (2000). Das Sportartenkonzept in Vergangenheit und Gegenwart. *Sportunterricht, 49,* 4–8.

Söll, W. (2005). *Sportunterricht – Sport unterrichten. Ein Handbuch für Sportlehrer* (6. edn.). Schorndorf: Hofmann.

Terhart, E. (2019). *Didaktik – Eine Einführung.* Stuttgart: Reclam.

Thiele, J., & Schierz, M. (2011). Handlungsfähigkeit – revisited. Plädoyer zur Wiederaufnahme einer didaktischen Leitidee. *Spectrum der Sportwissenschaft, 23*(1), 52–75.

Treutlein, G., Funke, J. & Sperle, N. (Eds.). (1992). *Körpererfahrung im Sport. Wahrnehmen – lernen Gesundheit fördern* (2., überarbeitete Aufl.). Aachen: Meyer & Meyer.

Volkamer, M. (1987). *Von der Last mit der Lust im Schulsport – Probleme der Pädagogisierung des Sports*. Schorndorf: Hofmann.

Volkamer, M., & Zimmer, R. (1984). „Was bleibt vom Sport im Schulsport?" In ADL (Eds.), *Schüler im Sport – Sport für Schüler* (pp. 226–232). Schorndorf: Hofmann.

Wopp, C. (2007). Lebenswelt, Jugendkulturen und Sport in der Schule. In R. Laging (Eds.), *Neues Taschenbuch des Sportunterrichts. Kompaktausgabe* (3., veränderte und korrigierte Aufl., pp. 104–122). Hohengehren: Schneider.

Zimmer, R. (1996). Psychomotorik in der Grundschule. In M. Polzin (Eds.), *Bewegung, Spiel und Sport in der Grundschule – Fachliche und fächerübergreifende Orientierung* (pp. 70–81). Frankfurt: AK Grundschule.

Zimmer, R. (2003). Wahrnehmen – Erleben – Bewegen. Psychomotorische Entwicklungsförderung. In G. Köppe, & J. Schwier (Eds.), Handbuch Grundschulsport (pp. 367–380). Hohengehren: Schneider.

Zimmer, R. (2019). *Handbuch Psychomotorik – Theorie und Praxis der psychomotorischen Förderung von Kindern* (14. edn.). Freiburg: Herder.

Methodological Basics

6

Abstract

This chapter deals with the methodological basics of physical education. Starting from considerations for understanding and systematizing methods in sports, methodological measures, methodological exercise series, and methodological procedures are presented as the basis of an object-oriented methodology. In contrast, the subject-oriented methodology emphasizes the educational claim of physical education and resorts to methodological types of staging. In the sense of an integrative view, the methodological spectrum in physical education is finally clarified. The chapter is supplemented by an excursion into movement tasks in physical education.

6.1 Introduction

Methodological questions deal with the concrete **staging of teaching-learning processes.** This addresses fundamental questions of mediation: "How should a teacher proceed in class? In what way should he support the students' learning and working process? What is the connection between the subject matter to be conveyed or worked on and the way in which a teacher structures the process of mediation or elaboration? What type of support is most advantageous for which students? [...] How large is the methodological scope that the reality of school and the everyday life of teaching offer the teacher?" (Terhart 2021, p. 47). If we summarize these general questions of the educational scientist Ewald Terhart, it is about the **manner of conveying** content or the **path to a goal** (cf. Kurz 2007). As is well known, there are many ways to Rome. This commonplace actually also applies to the methodological approach in teaching. However, the methodological path should be consciously chosen and justified.

This task is particularly challenging with regard to physical education. This is due, on the one hand, to the fact that the subject is very rich in prerequisites. Students have very different, positively or negatively charged prior experiences in relation to movement, games, and sports, which must be taken into account when staging the lessons (Neuber 2020). On the other hand, sports offerings in the sense of an **educational physical education** not only aim at conveying a (motor) content, but always at promoting overarching emotional, social, and cognitive skills and abilities (Prohl 2022). It is therefore not surprising that the **methodological topic in physical education** has always played a central role and filled entire textbook shelves in earlier times (e.g., Fetz 1961; Seybold-Brunnhuber 1972; Czwalina 1988). Since the 1990s, the topic has been discussed less sport(specific) and more cross-cutting, with the **matter of sport** or the **development of the subject** being in the foreground depending on the didactic approach (see Chap. 5). The methodological topic in sports also involves confirming one's position as a teacher in order to make justified decisions.

6.2   Basic Concepts

The task of teachers is not limited to imparting certain skills and abilities, attitudes and knowledge to their students. Rather, they should *stage*the lessons "with wit and imagination, with head, heart and hand" (Meyer 2009, p. 20). Accordingly, the **methodical action** of teachers is based on the purposeful organization, social interaction and meaningful communication with their students (Meyer 2009, p. 21). To this end, they use **teaching methods**, which are understood as forms of action with which teachers can pursue subject-specific and cross-curricular goals. They thus describe "a certain way of proceeding" (Terhart 2019, p. 181). Methodical decisions must be made at different **levels of methodical action**, such as the level of forms of action, social forms or teaching steps. For physical education, these levels are particularly complex because cognitive, social, motor and emotional goals are pursued here. The smallest methodical units in sports, such as the movement instruction, the movement task and the movement stimulation, are among the **methodical measures** (Heymen and Leue 2014, pp. 133–151).

The combination of several instructions or tasks for learning a sport-specific skill is referred to as a **methodical series**. Its structure usually follows methodical principles such as "From easy to difficult" or "From known to unknown" (Heymen and Leue 2014, pp. 156–160). If methodical measures and series are "summarized according to a higher-level aspect, this results in a **methodical procedure**" (Größing 2007, p. 209). A distinction is made between the inductive and deductive as well as the synthetic and analytical procedures. While the previous terms are rather oriented towards the mediation of the cause of sport, **types of staging** rather refer to the development of the subject. They highlight a certain activity in physical education, e.g. "presenting and showing" or "playing and discovering" (Laging 2000). This refers to the two basic **understandings of methods in sports**—the object-oriented and the subject-oriented methodology.

6.3 Foundations

The central decision dimensions in teaching are goals, content and methods. They answer the three central questions of "Why?" (goals), "What?" (content) and "How?" (methods) of the instruction. Usually, the "Why" and the "What" are attributed to the field of didactics and the "How" to the methodology (Terhart 2019, pp. 180–183). Nevertheless, goals, content and methods are in a specific reciprocal relationship in the sense of the **implementation context** (see Sect. 4.3), which can be differently pronounced depending on the conceptual understanding. Thus, the classical educational-theoretical didactics assumes a **primacy of didactics over methodology**, i.e. methodological questions are subordinated to questions of goals and content. At first glance, this seems understandable: First, the goals and content of a lesson are determined, then one considers how they should be conveyed. On second glance, however, there are also doubts: "The method constructs the object" and thus creates the decisive prerequisites for which goals can be achieved with which content (Kurz 2007, p. 12). From this, a **primacy of methodology over didactics** can certainly also be derived.

In a classical understanding, teaching methods are "recurring patterns of teaching activities that serve to convey teaching objectives and content, i.e., are intended to facilitate learning and can be applied by many teachers" (Einsiedler 1981, p. 17). In this **autonomous understanding of methods**, the goals and content precede the methodological decisions. In a more comprehensive view, the interactions of objectives, content, and methods are considered equally. This position is referred to as **didactic understanding of methods** (Kurz 2007, p. 16). In this broader understanding, the methodological actions of the students are also discussed (Terhart 2019, p. 181). A possible definition of teaching methods then refers to "the **forms and procedures,** in and with which teachers and students acquire the natural and societal reality surrounding them under institutional conditions" (Meyer 2009, p. 45). However, the teacher always has the responsibility for the use of the methods within the framework of instructional processes. The so-called **power of methods** thus lies with the teachers. In contrast to goals and content, which are more or less predetermined by guidelines and curricula, they can largely determine the methods themselves (cf. Kurz 2007).

The concept of **methodical action** by teachers can be understood as "staging of instruction through the purposeful organization of work, through social interaction and meaningful communication" with the students (Meyer 2009, p. 21). It is subject to the **antinomies of pedagogical action** in school (see Sect. 3.3): "Teaching methods are straitjacket and liberation in one. Their contradictoriness drives the teaching process forward" (Meyer 2009, p. 54). This means that teachers guide their instruction, but at the same time, students should engage more or less independently with the subject of instruction. The educationalist Benner (2001) calls this the **principle of external prompting for self-activity**. If one also includes the specific subject matter "movement, games and sports" with its subject-specific and cross-curricular demands, it becomes extremely complex. Perhaps this is one reason why many sports didactic works avoid a precise definition of the concept of method. Nevertheless, a definition is proposed here:

▶ **Methods in physical education** are forms of action used by physical education teachers to guide instruction and support their students in engaging with selected movement topics, thereby achieving subject-specific and cross-curricular objectives.

To make the complexity of the topic of methods manageable, different **levels of methodical action** are distinguished. For example, Meyer (2009, p. 115) differentiates between action situations, action patterns, teaching steps, social forms, and major methodological forms. These levels are of varying complexity. Action situations, for example, refer to a single task or feedback, while major methodological forms concern the basic design of a teaching scenario, such as a lesson, a course, or an excursion. However, these five levels can only be considered in context because they are mutually dependent. At the same time, methodological decisions do not take place in a "vacuum," but depend on the respective framework conditions. These **dimensions of the teaching method** are summarized by Terhart (2019, pp. 195–199) in a model that distinguishes four aspects: With regard to the learning object, it is the dimension "material encounter ," with regard to the institution school, the dimension "framing," with regard to the learners, the dimension "learning support," and with regard to the learning objective, the dimension "target achievement" (see Fig. 6.1). This model has also been applied to PE (Laging 2006; Pfitzner and Neuber 2012).

Similarly, the discussion about a new task culture, which arose in the aftermath of the "PISA shock" primarily in the so-called core subjects, was taken up by sports didactics. Within the framework of competence-oriented physical education, the **concept of the learning task** is of particular importance (Pfitzner 2014). A learning task can be understood as an arrangement of "meaningful, content-related and mutually coordinated tasks for learning" (Pfitzner and Aschebrock 2013, p. 3). It serves in particular the **cognitive activation** of students in physical education. Other demands include subject orientation, social interaction, the possibility of alternative solutions, and relevance to the real world (Pfitzner and Neuber 2022). It is beyond dispute that the perspective of the learning task has expanded the task discourse in sports didactics. In addition to cognitive activation, motor and **aesthetic activation** in physical education are also discussed (Laging 2022). Whether the learning task is a new type of task or whether the learning task merely extends the idea of the classic movement task (see Sect. 6.3.2) can be discussed (Neuber 2014).

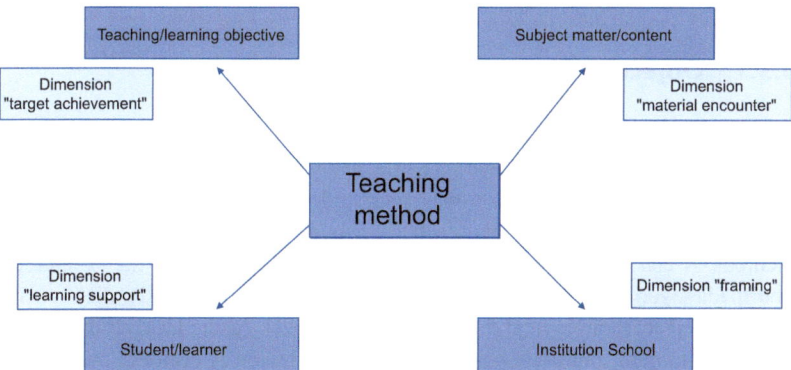

Fig. 6.1 Dimensions of the definition of teaching method. (Mod. according to Terhart 2019, p. 196)

▶ **Literature Tip** Pfitzner, M. (Ed.). (2014). *Aufgabenkultur im Sportunter-*
richt – Konzepte und Befunde zur Methodendiskussion für eine neue Lern-
kultur (Bildung und Sport, 5). Wiesbaden: Springer VS.
Michael Pfitzner combines numerous contributions to the task and
competence discourse in sports didactics in his anthology. This also
includes empirical studies in this field.

Ultimately, the **methodological decisions** of a teacher depend on the pedagogical orientation of the teaching and the associated didactic concept. In reference to
the two **tasks of pedagogical action** in PE (see Chap. 1) and the derived sports
didactic orientations (see Sect. 5.3), an object-oriented and a subject-oriented
methodology in sports can be distinguished (Köppe 2009). Such a **dichotomous
view** is quite common in the methodological field. For example, Zimmer (1994)
distinguishes the measures "instructing" and "stimulating". Kretschmer (1997)
speaks of "directing" and "offering" or in a later contribution of "instructing" and
"supervising" (Kretschmer 2000). Movement pedagogical approaches also use
this juxtaposition. Frequently cited, for example, is the "comprehensive teaching", which should be distinguished from "mediating teaching" (Funke-Wieneke
1995). The following also takes up the dual orientation of methodological action
in terms of an **object-oriented** and a **subject-oriented methodology**, before the
approaches are finally considered integratively.

6.3.1   Object-oriented Methodology

The object-oriented methodological understanding starts from the subject of
sport, which should be conveyed as effectively as possible. **Motor skills and
abilities** are prepared in such a way that students can learn them as smoothly
as possible. Ultimately, this approach follows an autonomous understanding of
methods. A classic object-oriented method model, developed by the "Bielefelder
Sportpädagogen" (sports pedagogues from the city of Bielefeld), distinguishes
five levels of methodological decisions (see Fig. 6.2): At the level of the **general
teaching concept**, the basic orientation of a PE lesson is decided: analytical or
holistic, deductive or inductive, closed or open (Kurz 2007, p. 18). At the level
of the **teaching steps**, it is about the temporal structure or sequence of the teaching steps. Typical for object-oriented method concepts is the methodical exercise
series for learning sport-specific skills (Söll 2005, pp. 123–128). The level of
social forms deals with the size of learning groups: individual work, pair work,

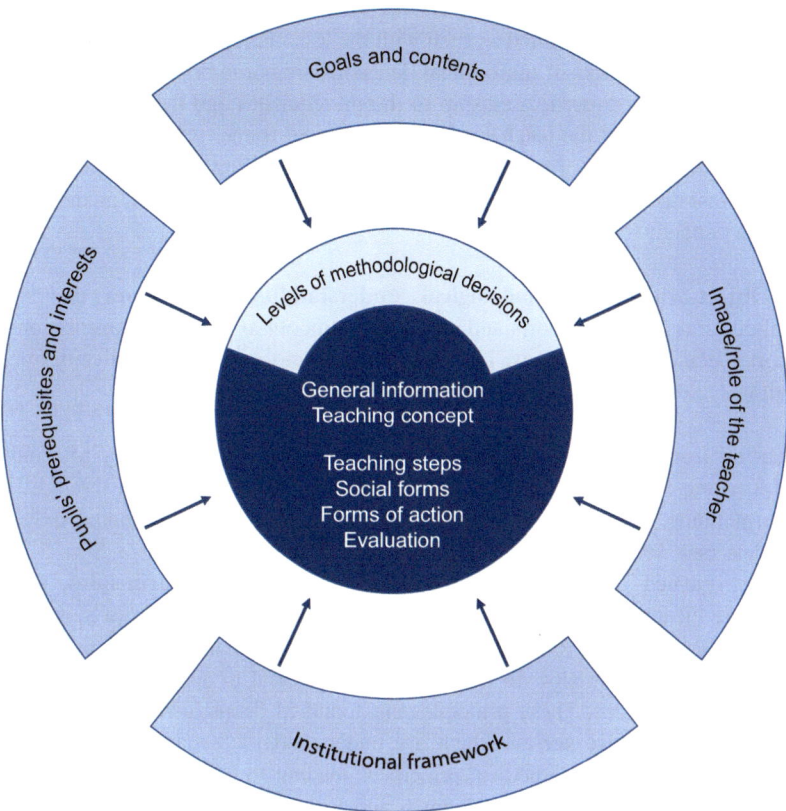

Fig. 6.2 Levels of methodical action. (Mod. according to Kurz 2007, p. 21)

small group work, work in the class community. Older method books also present "formation forms" (circle, row, alley, etc.) (Fetz 1988, pp. 240–257).

The level of **methodical measures**—Kurz (2007) speaks of "action forms"—refers to the smallest methodical units of PE teaching. These include movement instruction, movement task, movement regulation, movement correction, movement aid, movement description, movement explanation, etc. (Heymen and Leue 2014, pp. 133–151). Overall, action forms are impulses through which the teacher directly controls the lesson. The last level of the model is called **evaluation**. This includes all measures that provide information about the process and result of the lesson: "For us, decisions about forms of evaluation are part of the method and must be planned and justified as such with the lesson preparation" (Kurz 2007, p. 21). Overall, the **levels of methodical decisions** are not to be seen independently, but they are in a direct relationship to the prerequisites and interests of the students, to the role of the teacher, to the institutional framework of the school and last but not least to the goals and contents of a lesson (Kurz 2007, pp. 20–22).

Against the backdrop of the Bielefeld model, the object-oriented methodology can be defined:

▶ **Object-oriented methodological understandings** start from the societal-cultural reality of sports and aim at a as smooth as possible transmission of sport-specific action patterns. They are generally more closed-deductive in orientation.

Starting from the logic of standardized sports, these approaches try to remove all learning obstacles on the way to mastering a motor target form through lesson planning. In this respect, there is a certain proximity to planning didactic models (see Sect. 4.3.2) and object-oriented didactic concepts (see Sect. 5.3.1). Object-oriented understandings often refer to **methodical principles,** which structure the learning process. These include principles such as "From easy to difficult", "From simple to complex", "From known to unknown", "From low-risk to high-risk", "From slow to fast" or "From pictorial to abstract" (Sportjugend NRW 1998, p. 128). These principles are found as "construction principles" in **methodical exercise series**, which are understood as "sequences of exercises ordered according to methodical principles, leading to the learning of a specific motor skill (target exercise)" (Heymen and Leue 2014, p. 156). This is distinguished from **methodical game series,** which serve to introduce small or large sports games.

A special significance for the understanding of object-oriented methods is attributed to **methodical procedures** (see Fig. 6.3). They represent a fundamental teaching approach that is applied to an entire lesson. Typically, the "inductive" and "deductive" as well as the "synthetic" and "analytical" procedures are distinguished (Größing 2007, p. 209). The **inductive procedure** "emphasizes the independence and self-activity of the student and accepts detours in the learning process for this purpose" (Größing 2007, p. 209). Starting from a movement task, learners search for and test a suitable task solution, which is then highlighted, corrected, practiced, and applied (see Fig. 6.4). In contrast, the **deductive procedure** starts from a defined target exercise, which is described and demonstrated, and

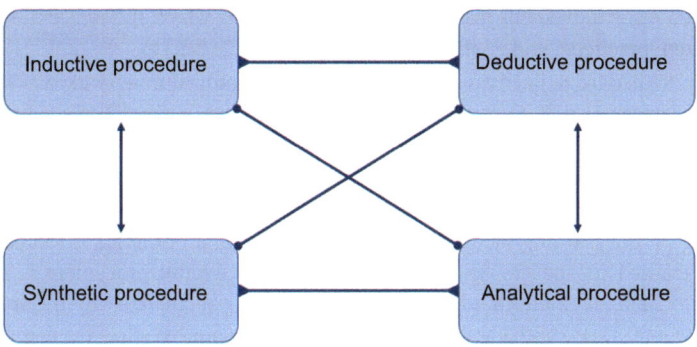

Fig. 6.3 Classic methodical procedures. (Mod. according to Größing 2007, p. 209)

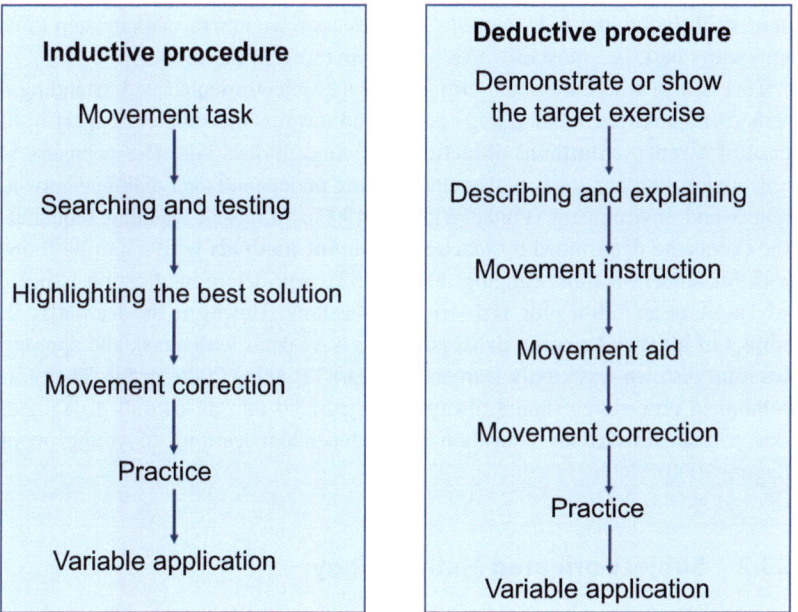

Fig. 6.4 Inductive vs. deductive teaching methods. (Mod. according to Größing 2007, p. 210)

relies on clear movement instructions, on the basis of which the target exercise is corrected, practiced, and applied (Größing 2007, pp. 210–211).

The **synthetic procedure**—also called holistic procedure—is used whenever a target exercise can be learned "in one go" or when a breakdown into partial movements does not seem sensible. For difficult movement sequences, "aids can be used to facilitate the execution of the movement for the student" (Heymen and Leue 2014, p. 129). The **analytical procedure**—also known as elemental procedure or partial learning method—is used when the target exercise is too complex to be learned in one go. Sometimes, however, the overall movement is broken down to such an extent that the target exercise is not recognized by the students. The inductive and synthetic procedures have a certain proximity. They are generally considered to be more student-oriented. Likewise, the deductive and analytical procedures have certain overlaps. They are generally considered to be more subject-oriented (Größing 2007, pp. 209–214). Overall, all four methods, according to this understanding, primarily aim at the **learning of a standardized movement skill.** Individual task solutions are only seen as an intermediate step to the supposedly best, i.e., most effective solution in terms of the sport.

This is also where the main criticism of the object-oriented understanding of methods begins: The methodology is oriented towards the subject of sport in the sense of a **representational didactics**. The concept does not offer openness for subjective solutions, nor is movement learning understood as a dialogue between subject and environment (Funke-Wieneke 1997). In closed teaching sequences, "the events are determined by **teacher-dominant methods** with a narrow framework for student action" (Laging 2006, p. 52). Self-determined action is not or only used as an "alibi" for skill-oriented teaching. However, the learner is the **subject of his own learning process,** "he actively deals with a task and appropriates it in 'his own way': only learners can learn" (Laging 2006, p. 54). Therefore, methodical procedures should always be integrated into an overall pedagogical concept that aims at the education and independent learning of young people (Laging 2000).

6.3.2 Subject-oriented Methodology

The subject-oriented understanding of methods starts from the subject or the **learning process of the subject**. Therefore, the decision for a specific method in physical education is "not only to be made within a complex mixture of goals and contents of the lesson, but also in relation to a pedagogical self-understanding of learning and education" (Laging 2000, p. 3). In this respect, the focus of this approach is less on the matter of sports with its more or less standardized skills, but rather on the individual experience and the **meaningful connections of movement** in a subjectively significant action context (Scherer 1999). The understanding of movement underlying this approach is described by Trebels (1999, p. 197) as "engaging with the task and a vigilant understanding of the connection between sensing and effecting in action". Against this background, the subject-oriented understanding of methods is not only about a student-oriented teaching of a subject, but the method is also the goal, i.e. students should also acquire a **methodological competence** in physical education. "Therefore, learning itself is at the center—learning should be learned" (Laging 2000, p. 5). In this sense, the approach explicitly follows a didactic understanding of methods (see Sect. 6.3).

▶ **Literature Tip** Laging, R. (2006). *Methodisches Handeln im Sportunterricht – Grundzüge einer bewegungspädagogischen Unterrichtslehre*. Seelze: Kallmeyer.
   Ralf Laging provides a comprehensive overview of the topic of methods in physical education in his volume. He takes a subject-oriented perspective.

A method model for the subject-oriented understanding of methods has been presented by Ralf Laging (2000) (see Fig. 6.5). It distinguishes five levels of methodical action, which are embedded in the framework conditions of school and teaching as well as in the personal and situational conditions of the learning group. In contrast to the object-oriented method model, the methods are not only framed by the underlying **teaching concepts**, but also by the **educational claim and understanding of learning,** which underlies the chosen concept. The orientation towards the learning process of the students leads to "an open, holistic, action-oriented and student-active concept of physical education" (Laging 2000, p. 6). The starting point of the model are concrete **action situations** of the lesson. They are stimulated by specific **action patterns,** such as movement instruction, movement task or movement stimulation. The temporal structuring of a lesson takes place at the level of the **teaching steps:** "At the core, it is about designing a meaningful sequence of action situations directed towards the goal of the teaching/learning unit" (Laging 2000, p. 7).

At the level of **social and differentiation forms**, the cooperation in the class is determined, but at the same time it is also about controlling the relationships between teachers and learners. The level of **major methodological forms** concerns the overarching staging of the lesson, for example in the form of plans, projects or courses. Overall, the model of a subject-oriented understanding of

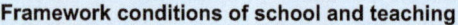

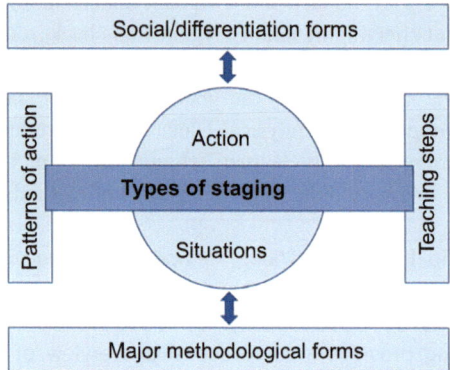

Fig. 6.5 Levels of methodical action. (Mod. according to Laging 2000, p. 7)

methods is based on the methodological ideas of the didactician Hilbert Meyer (2009). From him, Laging also adopts the term staging, which stands as a connecting element in the center of the model. Action patterns, teaching steps, social and differentiation forms as well as major methodological forms are summarized in so-called **types of staging** of the lesson. The term staging is found "in the didactic literature wherever it is about a relatively complex 'whole view' of the design of instructional teaching/learning situations" (Laging 2000, p. 8). Types of staging highlight a central methodical action, which determines the course of the lesson. **Types of staging in physical education** can be, for example, "presenting and showing", "building and constructing" or "playing and discovering" (Laging 2000, p. 8).

Based on Ralf Laging's method model, the subject-oriented methodology can be defined.

▶ **Subject-oriented methodological understandings** start from the individual possibilities and desires of the individual and aim at the development of the subject. They tend to be more open-inductive in nature.

The subject-oriented understanding of methods emerged primarily within the context of critical-emancipatory concepts for physical education in the 1980s and 90s, for example within the framework of the dialogical movement concept or the body experience concept (Neuber 2021, pp. 31–50). Methodologically, this also developed a **counter-movement** to traditional "instruction, teaching and training methods" in sports (Funke-Wieneke 2009, p. 319). However, the roots of the subject-oriented methodology go back to the **reform pedagogical physical education** of the 1920s. As an alternative to the "learning school" of the Wilhelmine imperial era, reform pedagogy emphasized the immediacy and naturalness of learning in a "life school". From this time comes, for example, the **Natural Gymnastics ("Natürliches Turnen"),** which can be traced back to Karl Gaulhofer and Margarete Streicher. Their child-friendly movement training was based on the principle of "preserving and developing the natural movements of children" (Prohl 2006, p. 47). In this context, they worked less with instructions and more with tasks. The **movement task** was already considered a particularly good methodological measure at that time, "because it does not destroy the holistic character of the activity and because various changes in the movement sequence are possible without being specifically demanded" (Streicher 1961, p. 13).

Movement Tasks in Physical Education
The movement task is one of the most important, if not *the* most important methodological measure for steering physical education. As an invitation to students to independently solve a specific motion problem, the movementtask provides a framework for action, but in principle allows for different solutions (Neuber 2000, pp. 117–118). It is usually less about achieving a certain, "best" target form than about trying out and developing one's own movement possibilities. All solutions are considered "correct" as long as the minimum requirements formulated in the task are met (Stoßberg and Datzer 1985, pp. 68–70). In the methodological spectrum between instructions that only allow one solution and stimulations that are completely open, the movement task serves a mediating function (Neuber 2010). Nevertheless, the movement task—like other methodological measures—depends on the educational context in which it is used (Laging 2006,

pp. 59–70). At least three approaches to the motion task can be identified: A sports-oriented, an artistic-educational, and a movement-educational interpretation (cf. Neuber 2014).

Within the framework of the **sports-oriented interpretation**, the movement task is given a place in the context of the inductive teaching procedure (Größing 2007, 195–196). The goal is to learn sports motor skills as smoothly as possible. Although the motion task is also credited with effects in the areas of social learning, cognitive understanding, or creative design, the "quick and sure path to the learning result" must be postponed for this (Größing 2007, p. 195). The **artistic-educational interpretation** of the movement task aims at developing one's own movement and expression possibilities (Neuber 2002). The decisive factor for this is the definition of degrees of freedom in the task. The pedagogical challenge is to avoid falling into arbitrariness or dirigisme during the "walk on the narrow ridge between openness and guidance" (Stoßberg 1984, p. 336). In addition to differentiating between the closedness and openness of tasks, gradations are also made with regard to complexity. The so-called **unconventional motion task** aims at inventing new, unusual movement possibilities and is intended to stimulate engagement with "never-seen-before" or "otherwise not occurring" (Tiedt 1991, p. 68). A distinction is also made between tasks on the motor and the acting level (see Fig. 6.6).

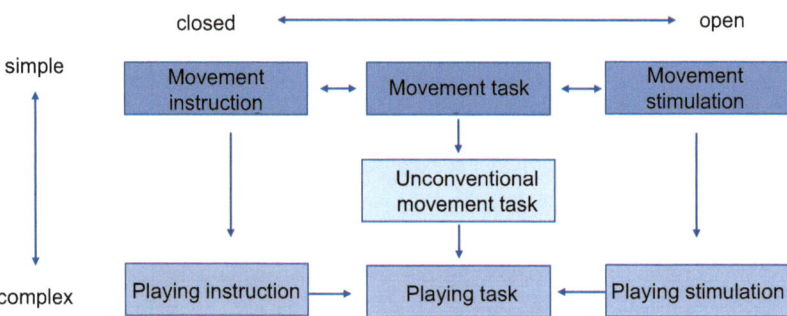

Fig. 6.6 Movement tasks in the context of the artistic-educational approach. (Mod. according to Neuber 2000, p. 120)

In the **movement-educational interpretation** of the movement task, it is not only about finding one's own movement and expression possibilities, but also "about the self-interpreted and co-designed movement action as a solution to the posed movement problem", i.e., a new approach to the subject "movement" (Laging 2006, p. 64). This means that movement is fundamentally understood in a context of meaning that consists of at least an "actor", i.e., a subject that moves, a specific situation in which the movement action is embedded, and a meaning that guides the movement and gives it structure (Trebels 1992). In this respect, the motion task puts "the perspective and the **learning process of the learner** itself at the center of consideration" (Laging 2006, p. 63). Against the backdropof these three interpretations, the movement task can be understood as a central, "native" measure for staging physical education lessons.

Even the **subject-oriented methodological understanding** is not without criticism. Representatives of an object-oriented approach, for example, complain that students must test all inductively developed movement patterns until they decide on the "best solution". This takes time "and strains the patience of teachers and students alike" (Söll 2005, p. 201). Somewhat more fundamental is the criticism from an educational-theoretical perspective: "There is a strange and unfounded **technology syndrome** in current pedagogy. [...] Even the attempt to convert more general units and findings into manageable procedural and art rules of education and teaching inevitably attracts the accusation of overlooking the true needs and motives of the learners with technocratic cold-heartedness and making the educators into mere assistants of soulless machines" (Prange 1986, p. 11). Indeed, the question of the pros and cons of **methodical exercise series** is still controversial: Is it useful for students to learn the basics of the crawl flip turn quickly and smoothly using a methodical serie, or do they have to work out these movement patterns in an open process themselves?

6.4   Overview of Methodological Basics

Methods in physical education are forms of action that PE teachers use to control their teaching and thus promote their students. In contrast to the largely curricular obligation of goals and contents, the method offers teachers certain **scope for decision:** "Since the method first makes the content a topic and thus decides on the chances of achieving the goal, this power of the teacher is not small" (Kurz 2007, p. 13). Teachers should be aware of this power and use it in the sense of **pedagogical responsibility**. This also means standing by methodical decisions—such as strenuous practice or open experimentation—and enduring them: "Constructive, responsible effects can only be drawn from **uncertainty**" (Erdmann 1992, p. 78). Therefore, it is not trivial whether teachers opt for an object-oriented methodology and thus essentially follow the logic of standardized sports, or whether they prefer a subject-oriented methodology and thus put the individual movement needs of children and adolescents in the foreground (Köppe 2009).

Both decisions are potentially associated with certain advantages and disadvantages (see Table 6.1). The **object-oriented methodological understanding** refers to sport as a social practice and thus primarily follows the "principle of appropriateness to the subject matter" (Benner 2001). This leads to comparatively clear teaching paths and a high transparency of physical education. The learners know what is expected of them. At the same time, their individual movement needs are sometimes neglected, and the PE teachers often act very dominantly. The **subject-oriented methodological understanding** starts with the individual movement needs of the students and thus particularly emphasizes the "principle of external demand for self-activity" (Benner 2001). The teaching paths of physical education are open and communication-oriented. The relationship between teachers and learners is partnership-based. However, this can also lead to a neglect of sport as a social practice, because teachers, in the sense of a protective teaching style, shy away from the imposition of practicing and training.

Ultimately, physical education teachers are always challenged to make the "right" **methodological decisions** against the backdrop of the prerequisites and goals of a teaching situation. It can help to realize that they can design the lessons

Table 6.1 Object- vs. subject-oriented methodological understanding. (According to Köppe 2009)

Object-oriented understanding of methods	Subject-oriented understanding of methods
Orientation towards sport as a social practice	Consideration of individual (movement) needs
Principle of appropriateness	Principle of encouraging independence
Clear communication channels	Open, communication-oriented mediation channels
Transparency of physical education	Partnership-based teacher-student relationship
Neglect of individual (movement) needs	Neglect of sport as a social practice
Dominance of sports teachers	Protective teaching style

more closed or open depending on the situation (Funke 1991). There are gradual nuances between the basic positions of "object orientation" and "subject orientation", which can be interpreted as more closed or open depending on the requirement. An integrative approach that overcomes usual dichotomous understandings lies in the idea of a **methodological spectrum** between a closed and an open teaching staging, which goes back to methodological considerations on creative movement education (Neuber 2010). At the level of methodological procedures, a teaching by instructing, a teaching by tasking, and a teaching by stimulating are distinguished. The procedures are accompanied at the level of methodological measures by the movement instruction, the movement task, and the movement stimulation (see Table 6.2).

The **teaching by instructing** aim at the mediation of more or less standardized movement forms and in its pure form allows only one correct movement solution. The teachers prescribe this movement form through movement instructions, explanations, and demonstrations and correct them if necessary. The working method is deductively oriented towards the given movement forms and is product-oriented. On the other side of the spectrum is the **teaching by stimulating**. It explicitly aims at own forms of moving and thus allows unlimited solution possibilities. The central measure is the movement stimulation. The approach is inductive and process-oriented. Between these two extremes lies the **teaching by tasking**. It aims at the development of diverse movement forms. In the sense of the movement task, there is more than one possible solution for a task. However, the procedure can also end with an individual movement form, as it can lead to an objectively meaningful, e.g., effective movement form. Thus, the procedure is both deductive and inductive as well as process and product-oriented.

Table 6.2 Methodological procedures. (According to Neuber 2010, p. 468)

Teaching by instructing	Teaching by tasking	Teaching by stimulating
Standardized forms of movement	Diverse forms of movement	Own forms of movement
One possible solution	Many possible solutions	Unlimited possible solutions
Movement instruction	Movement task	Movement stimulation
Deductive	Deductive and inductive	Inductive
Product orientation	Process and product orientation	Process orientation

1. Why are the teaching methodological challenges in PE particularly complex?
2. What distinguishes the autonomous and didactic understanding of methods?
3. What does it mean that the power of methods lies with the teachers?
4. To what extent do the dimensions of a teaching method influence the concrete staging of the lesson?
5. What distinguishes object-oriented and subject-oriented methodologies in PE?
6. How is it to be understood that the methodological measures represent the smallest methodological units in sports?
7. How do the inductive and deductive procedures relate to the synthetic and analytical procedures?
8. What is meant by types of staging in physical education?
9. Why is the movement task considered the most important methodological measure in sports?
10. To what extent can physical education teachers draw on a methodological spectrum?

References

Benner, D. (2001). *Allgemeine Pädagogik – eine systematisch-problemgeschichtliche Einführung in die Grundstruktur pädagogischen Denkens und Handels* (4., völlig neue bearbeitete Aufl.). Weinheim, München: Juventa.

Czwalina, C. (Eds.). (1988). *Methodisches Handeln im Sportunterricht – Analysen und Reflexionen zur Methodik in der Sportdidaktik.* Schorndorf: Hofmann.

Einsiedler, W. (1981). *Lehrmethoden: Probleme und Ergebnisse der Lehrmethodenforschung.* München: Urban & Schwarzberg.

Erdmann, R. (1992). Theorie ohne Praxis ist leer – Praxis ohne Theorie ist blind. Plädoyer für die Unsicherheit in zehn Thesen. In R. Erdmann (Eds.), *Alte Fragen neu gestellt – Anmerkungen zu einer zeitgemäßen Sportdidaktik* (pp. 69–80). Schorndorf: Hofmann.

Fetz, F. (1961). *Allgemeine Methodik der Leibesübungen* (1. edn.). Wien: Österreich. Bundesverlag.

Fetz, F. (1988). *Allgemeine Methodik der Leibesübungen* (9. edn.). Frankfurt: Limpert.

Funke, J. (1991). Unterricht öffnen – offener unterrichten. *Sportpädagogik, 15*(2), 12–18.

Funke-Wieneke, J. (1995). Vermitteln – Schritte zu einem ökologischen Unterrichtskonzept. *Sportpädagogik, 19*(5),10–17.

Funke-Wieneke, J. (1997). Von der „Körpererfahrung" zur „Thematisierung der Leiblichkeit". *Sporterziehung in der Schule* (1), 19–22.

Funke-Wieneke, J. (2009). Körpererfahrung. In H. Haag, & A. Hummel (Eds.), *Handbuch Sportpädagogik* (2., erweiterte Auflage, pp. 314–322). Schorndorf: Hofmann.

Größing, S. (2007). *Einführung in die Sportdidaktik – Lehren und Lernen im Sportunterricht* (9., überarbeitete und erweiterte Aufl.). Wiebelsheim: Limpert.

Heymen, N., & Leue, W. (2014). *Planung von Sportunterricht* (8., unveränderte Aufl.). Hohengehren: Schneider.

Köppe, G. (2009). Methoden. In H. Haag & A. Hummel (Eds.), *Handbuch Sportpädagogik* (2., erweiterte Aufl., pp. 198–205). Schorndorf: Hofmann.

Kretschmer, J. (1997). Akzente kindgerechter Bewegungserziehung. In E. Balz & P. Neumann (Eds.), *Wie pädagogisch soll der Schulsport sein?* (pp. 169–184). Schorndorf: Hofmann.

Kretschmer, J. (2000). Betreuen und Unterweisen. In P. Wolters, H. Ehni, J. Kretschmer, K. Scherler & W. Weichert, *Didaktik des Schulsports* (pp. 121–143). Schorndorf: Hofmann.

Kurz, D. (2007). Worum geht es in einer Methodik des Sportunterrichts? In Bielefelder Sportpädagogen, *Methoden im Sportunterricht – ein Lehrbuch in 14 Lektionen* (5. edn., pp. 9–24). Schorndorf: Hofmann.

Laging, R. (2000). *Methoden im Sportunterricht.* Sportpädagogik, *24*(5), 2–9.

Laging, R. (2006). *Methodisches Handeln im Sportunterricht – Grundzüge einer bewegungspädagogischen Unterrichtslehre.* Seelze: Kallmeyer.

Laging, R. (2022). Bewegung als Aufgabe. *Zeitschrift für sportpädagogische Forschung, 10*(1), 28–51.

Meyer, H. (2009). Unterrichtsmethoden (I: Theorieband, 14. edn.). Berlin: Cornelsen.

Neuber, N. (2000). *Kreativität und Bewegung – Grundlagen kreativer Bewegungserziehung und empirische Befunde* (Schriften der Deutschen Sporthochschule, 45). St. Augustin: Academia.

Neuber, N. (2002). Bewegung als gestaltbares Material – Der künstlerisch-pädagogische Ansatz der Bewegungserziehung. *Sportunterricht, 51*, 363–369.

Neuber, N. (2010). Darstellen, Vorführen, Aufführen – vom Bewegungsspiel zum Bewegungstheater. In H. Lange & S. Sinning (Eds.), *Handbuch Methoden im Sport – Lehren und Lernen in der Schule, im Verein und im Gesundheitssport* (pp. 458–476). Balingen: Spitta.

Neuber, N. (2014). Bewegungsaufgaben als Lernaufgaben? – Ansatzpunkte für eine zeitgemäße Aufgabenkultur im Schulsport. In M. Pfitzner (Eds.), Aufgabenkultur im Sportunterricht – Konzepte und Befunde zur Methodendiskussion für eine neue Lernkultur (Bildung und Sport, 5, pp. 41–64). Wiesbaden: Springer VS.

Neuber, N. (2020). *Fachdidaktische Konzepte Sport – Zielgruppen und Voraussetzungen* (Basiswissen Lernen im Sport). Wiesbaden: Springer VS. https://doi.org/10.1007/978-3-658-28464-0.

Neuber, N. (2021). *Fachdidaktische Konzepte Sport II – Themenfelder und Perspektiven* (Basiswissen Lernen im Sport). Wiesbaden: Springer VS. https://doi.org/10.1007/978-3-658-30249-8.

Pfitzner, M. (Eds.). (2014). *Aufgabenkultur im Sportunterricht – Konzepte und Befunde zur Methodendiskussion für eine neue Lernkultur* (Bildung und Sport, 5). Wiesbaden: Springer VS.

Pfitzner, M., & Neuber, N. (2012). Individuelle Förderung im Sport – Didaktisch-methodische Grundlagen. In N. Neuber & M. Pfitzner (Eds.), *Individuelle Förderung im Sport – Pädagogische Grundlagen und didaktisch-methodische Konzepte* (Begabungsforschung, 14, pp. 75–95). Münster: Lit.

Pfitzner, M., & Aschebrock, H. (2013). Aufgabenkultur – Voraussetzungen und Merkmale eines kompetenzorientierten Unterrichts. *Sportpädagogik, 37*(5), 2–6.

Pfitzner, M., & Neuber, N. (2022). Aufgabenkultur im Sport – von Lern- und Bewegungsaufgaben. In R. Sygusch, J. Hapke, S. Liebl & C. Töpfer (Eds.), *Kompetenzorientierung im Sport – Grundlagen, Modellentwurf und Anwendungsbeispiele* (pp. 68–86). Schorndorf: Hofmann.

Prange, K. (1986). *Bauformen des Unterrichts* (2. edn.). Bad Heilbrunn: Klinkhardt.

Prohl, R. (2006). *Grundriss der Sportpädagogik* (2. edn.). Wiebelsheim: Limpert.

Prohl, R. (2022). Der Doppelauftrag des Erziehenden Sportunterrichts. In V. Scheid & R. Prohl (Eds.), *Sportdidaktik – Grundlagen, Vermittlungsformen, Bewegungsfelder* (3., durchgesehene und korrigierte Aufl., pp. 64–84). Wiebelsheim: Limpert.

Scherer, H.-G. (1999). Lernen und Lehren von Bewegung. In B. Heinz & R. Laging (Eds.), *Bewegungslernen in Erziehung und Bildung* (pp. 27–38). Hamburg: Czwalina.

Seybold-Brunnhuber, A. (1972). *Didaktische Prinzipien der Leibeserziehung.* Schorndorf: Hofmann.

Söll, W. (2005). *Sportunterricht – Sport unterrichten* (6., unveränderte Aufl.). Schorndorf: Hofmann.

Sportjugend NRW (1998). Didaktische Grundlagen und methodische Grundlagen (IB 5.1). In Sportjugend NRW (Eds.), *Jugendarbeit im Sport – Materialien zur Qualifizierung von Mitarbeiterinnen und Mitarbeitern, Band 5: Planungsaspekte von sportlichen, kulturellen und politischen Vereinsangeboten* (pp. 1–140). Duisburg: Sportjugend NRW.

Stoßberg, B. (1984). Offene Bewegungsaufgaben – Möglichkeitsräume für Bewegungshandeln und Probleme ihrer Nutzung. *Sportunterricht, 33,* 335–342.

Stoßberg, B., & Datzer, E. (1985). Die Arbeit mit offenen Bewegungsaufgaben als Schlüssel zum selbständigen Gestalten im künstlerisch-pädagogischen Bereich des Sports. In H.-G. Artus (Eds.), *Handeln in Gymnastik/Tanz* (pp. 64–100). Bremen: Hochschulverlag.

Streicher, M. (1961). Die Bewegungsaufgabe. In M. Streicher (Eds.), *Natürliches Turnen* (Band V, 2. Aufl.). Wien: Verlag für Jugend und Volk.

Terhart, E. (2019). *Didaktik – Eine Einführung.* Stuttgart: Reclam.

Terhart, E. (2021). *Didaktische Theorien und Modelle.* Hagen: Fernuniversität.

Tiedt, W. (1991). Bewegungstheater. In Kultusministerium NRW (Eds.), *Sporttheater im Verein* (Materialien zum Sport in Nordrhein-Westfalen, 32, pp. 64–74). Frechen: Ritterbach.

Trebels, A. (1992). Das dialogische Bewegungskonzept – Eine pädagogische Auslegung von Bewegung. *Sportunterricht, 41,* 20–29.

Trebels, A. (1999). Sich-Bewegen: Lernen und Lehren – Anthropologisch-philosophische Orientierungen. In B. Heinz & R. Laging (Eds.), *Bewegungslernen in Erziehung und Bildung* (pp. 39–52). Hamburg: Czwalina.

Zimmer, R. (1994). *Handbuch der Bewegungserziehung – Didaktisch-methodische Grundlagen und Ideen für die Praxis* (3. edn.). Freiburg: Herder.

Individual Support

7

Abstract

This chapter deals with the concept of individual support in PE. Starting from a pedagogical understanding of diagnosis and support, two concepts for individual support *of* sports are presented with remedial teaching in physical education and talent support in sports. They are supplemented by learning support through movement and psychomotor development support in the sense of individual support *through* sports. Overall, an integrative concept for subject-specific and cross-curricular learning in sports is presented. An exkursion on development support in PE complements the chapter.

7.1 Introduction

Pedagogical action is aimed at supporting people. Regardless of the specific area in which one operates, pedagogical activity always aims to make "the educatee better, more capable, more efficient, more perfect or more valuable in some respect" (Brezinka 1990, p. 90). This also applies to the field of movement, games and sports, where the dual mandate of school sports has even anchored **development promotion** as a guiding idea (see Sect. 3.3.3). However, the promotion here only refers to one aspect of education and formation, namely the personal development of students. The concept of **Individual Support** is broader and also includes subject-specific learning. In the context of discussions about a new learning culture, the term has gained particular significance (Fischer 2014). As a result of national and international school performance studies (e.g. PISA,

© The Author(s), under exclusive license to Springer Fachmedien Wiesbaden Gmbh, part of Springer Nature 2025
N. Neuber, *Didactics of Physical Education and Sport*,
https://doi.org/10.1007/978-3-658-47188-0_7

TIMSS), it has become an educational policy term that has not only found its way into numerous decrees and school laws, but also significantly influences the practical work of educational institutions. Individual promotion has thus become a central **quality feature of "good teaching"**, if not even "good school".

The idea of promotion initially only referred to children and adolescents with special needs, e.g. with learning difficulties or a migration background. However, the understanding has now expanded. The concept of **Individual Promotion** today aims to "give every student [...] the chance to fully develop his or her motor, intellectual, emotional and social potential [...] and to support him or her with suitable measures" (Eckert 2016, p. 97). The promotion is closely related to the **individual diagnosis,** with the help of which the appropriate promotion measure should be determined. With this comprehensive understanding at the latest, individual promotion also becomes interesting for sports, not least because it addresses special **needs for promotion** as well as special **talents** (Pfitzner and Neuber 2020). In addition to educational physical education, the approach offers good starting points in the sense of an integrative sports didactic **concept of great range** (see Sect. 5.3), which is compatible with the school pedagogical promotion debate. However, dealing with strengths and weaknesses, competencies and deficits of students should be well considered.

7.2   Basic Concepts

The concept of individual support is based on a close interplay of diagnosis and support. A **diagnosis** serves to capture learning processes and learning outcomes as objectively as possible in order to improve individual learning of students on this basis (Ingenkamp and Lissmann 2008). Thus, pedagogical diagnostics are not primarily aimed at grading. The term **support** is understood in the broadest sense as the support of learning and personality development of children and adolescents (Fischer 2014). The **individual support** adopts this understanding and explicitly includes the individual needs and prerequisites of each individual student (Kunze 2016, p. 19). Behind this is the idea of **potential orientation,** which is intended to help unfold individual abilities and talents—the potential of a person—to the best possible extent. This is associated with the conviction that *every* person has potentials that need to be discovered and promoted (Fischer and Fischer-Ontrup 2020).

While individual support includes both subject-specific and non-subject-specific learning, **developmental support** emphasizes non-subject-specific learning or the personality development of adolescents (Neuber 2007). In this sense, the term is also understood in the dual mandate for school sports. Both support intentions in school face the problem that teachers can only focus on individual students to a limited extent in larger learning groups. From a methodological point of view, **differentiation** is therefore of central importance, i.e., the use of measures and tasks that are as precise as possible for each student (Heymann 2010). Closely related to this is the **individualization** of teaching, i.e., the pursuit of individual learning goals and paths. Ultimately, this can only succeed in school learning groups if the students take responsibility for their own learning process. In the sense of **self-regulated learning**, "learners independently plan, monitor and control their learning process and thus take an active role" (Fischer and Fischer-Ontrup 2020, p. 227).

7.3 Foundations

The term individual support became a central educational policy term in a short time following the "PISA shock" at the beginning of the 2000s. In doing so, educational policy and educational science are responding to massively changed **framework conditions for education and teaching** (Fischer 2014). Demographic change and immigration, social modernization processes and new labor market structures not only lead to increasingly heterogeneous learning groups, but also to changed competence expectations for the upcoming generation (see Sect. 2.3). Added to this at the beginning of the 2020s were the massive learning deficits of children and adolescents as a result of the **COVID-19 pandemic.** Numerous, sometimes hastily developed "catch-up packages" explicitly relied on the idea of individual diagnosis and support to close the gaps in the so-called main subjects as quickly as possible (Zierer 2021). In fact, individual support aims "at the optimal design of individual learning processes, so that support and learning are directly related" (Fischer 2014, p. 25). **Educational success**, however, cannot be planned linearly, let alone methodically controlled. Moreover, it is not very helpful to reduce learning to a few cognitive learning objects and to ignore all other areas of development, such as physical and social ones (Laging 2017).

Even though the concept of **individual support** is currently in vogue, the idea is not new. "Dedicated teachers have always strived to turn to each individual student, to accept them as autonomous, unique, and self-willed personalities, to accompany and support them on their not always easy path through school to adulthood" (Kunze and Solzbacher 2016, p. 9). Initially, the term was rather teacher-centered: "One can support someone (a talent, a person in need) or one can support something (a school, a charitable institution, an ideal concern), but one cannot support oneself. Thus, support implies **a need for support**" (Kunze

2016, p. 22). Nevertheless, individual support in a class will hardly succeed if students do not take responsibility for their learning process. Accordingly, the idea of **self-regulated learning** "is gaining in importance, especially since this format fulfills the claim that the learning environment recognizes the learners as its main participants, promotes their active participation, and develops in them an understanding of their own activity as learners" (Fischer and Fischer-Ontrup 2020, p. 227). Against this backdrop, the term can be defined.

▶ **Individual support** includes all actions by teachers and students "that are carried out with the intention or have the effect of supporting the learning of the individual student, taking into account their specific learning prerequisites, needs, paths, goals, and possibilities" (Kunze 2016, p. 22).

In terms of pedagogical action, individual support takes place in an **interactive mediation relationship** between teachers and students, which is accompanied by differences in competence, knowledge, and power. The relationship is tense, the fundamental asymmetry is insurmountable (see Sect. 3.3). Pedagogical action usually also aims at a larger learning group, which means that teachers have to rely on generally valid, more or less secured **rules** to shape their actions. On the other hand, the diversity of students requires consideration of the special conditions of the **individual case,** which cannot be subordinated to any general rule. Thus, individual support is fundamentally in a tension between abstract rule knowledge and concrete case reference (Helsper, 2010), with the individual case taking precedence in this concept.

▶   Literature Tip Fischer, C. (2014). *Individuelle Förderung als schulische Herausforderung*. Berlin: Friedrich-Ebert-Stiftung.
        In this expertise, Christian Fischer provides a condensed overview of the concept of individual support in Germany, also addressing the inclusion debate, qualification opportunities, and international perspectives.

While individual support in school was initially limited to so-called remedial teaching, it is now also used in regular teaching in the sense of individualized learning (Graumann 2008). Against the backdrop of the heterogeneity debate in school (Neuber 2020, pp. 93–114), individual support is intended to contribute to **educational justice**. It targets both lower-performing students with specific impairments and higher-performing students with specific talents (Fischer and Fischer-Ontrup 2020, p. 223). The support can thus lie both in the **compensation** of deficits, e.g., overcoming learning blocks, and in the expansion of competencies, e.g., the **acquisition of special expertise,**. However, starting with the deficits or competencies of the learners leads to a different design of the support offers. While proponents of the **deficit hypothesis** focus on compensating for weaknesses, as in traditional remedial teaching, proponents of the **competence hypothesis** emphasize the developmental potential of students (Neuber 2020, p. 40). Against this background, the two core terms "diagnosis" and "support" can be further defined.

▶ **Diagnosis** means "judging based on predefined categories, terms, or concepts—such as statements about how capable, competent, motivated, aggressive, or anxious someone is" (Helmke 2003, p. 92). The educational benefit of diagnostically obtained information lies in the verification and control of teaching actions.

In this respect, educational diagnosis is understood as part of teaching. Teachers often perform **diagnostic services,** both implicitly during teaching and as "punctual, detached from the immediate teaching process and explicit forms of information acquisition and processing" (Schrader 1989, p. 16). Diagnosis has only indirectly to do with the evaluation of students in terms of grading. Its primary importance is for the teaching actions of the teachers. Accordingly, the term support diagnosis is also used (Arnold et al. 2008). In educational research, **diagnostic competence** is now understood in a broad sense. This includes, in addition to diagnostic knowledge and skills, the competence to adequately assess the abilities of students and the difficulty of tasks (Schrader and Helmke 2001).

▶ **Support** is considered an educational term that "has a positive connotation and is associated with […] a special appreciation of joint learning, acceptance of diversity, and a specific professional ethical attitude of teachers" (Hanke 2010, p. 1). Support aims, in the broadest sense, at promoting people.

The interplay of diagnosis and support is considered a circular process within the framework of **support concepts**. Here, "diagnosis serves the continuous determination of individual learning starting positions, while support focuses on the systematic implementation of suitable learning offers" (Fischer and Fischer-Ontrup 2020, p. 226). Ideally, individual learning objectives and paths can be formulated for each student, and an individual learning and support plan can be developed. Characteristic of this is an attitude of **potential orientation** with the aim of achieving optimal "development and unfolding of performance-related ability and personality potentials" in every child and adolescent (Fischer and Fischer-On-trup 2020, p. 227). Teachers generally support this concern, but there is often a lack of appropriate integration into school development processes. The **learning and teaching culture** of many schools is still strongly oriented towards the idea of the classic "learning school" (Knauder and Reisinger 2017). Therefore, it often remains the task of the individual teacher to "help students find their own learning path through suitable diagnosis, appreciative counseling, and moderation" (Oefner et al. 2009, p. 9). This task also applies to school sports.

Subject-didactic concepts for individual support in sports are still scarce. Initially, only a concept for diagnostics and individual support in PE for secondary levels I and II was developed (Oefner et al., 2009). Nevertheless, the idea of individual support presents itself as an integrative concept for school sports when various subject-didactic approaches are combined (Neuber and Pfitzner 2012; Pfitzner and Neuber 2012a). The starting point for this are the two tasks of pedagogical action in PE and thus the dual mandate for school sports (see Chap. 1 and Sect. 3.3.3). Starting from an education *for* sports, the intention to promote can refer to the **individual support** *of* **movement, games and sports**. The focus is then on the motor skills and abilities of the students. On the other hand, the intention to promote in the sense of an education *through* sports can focus on the **individual support** *through* **movement, games and sports**. Then, overarching abilities, e.g., basic functions of learning, or personality traits are in the foreground. In both cases, the approach can be more deficit- or competence-oriented (see Table 7.1). This matrix can be used as a starting point for a **sports didactic analysis and classification**. For this purpose, four selected concepts for individual support in sports will be presented in the following.

Table 7.1 Sports didactic starting points for individual support of and through movement, games and sports. (Mod. according to Pfitzner and Neuber 2012a, b, p. 78)

	Individual support of movement, games and sports	Individual support through movement, games and sport
Individual deficits as a starting point	Remedial teaching in physical education	Learning support through movement, games and sports
Individual skills as a starting point	Talent development programs	Psychomotor Development support

7.3.1 Individual Support of Sports

A concept of individual support, where motor skills and abilities are in the fore-ground, is the **remedial teaching in pyhsical education.** Its roots lie in "Ortho-pedic School Gymnastics," which was developed at the beginning of the 20th century to promote children with physical performance weaknesses. This evolved into "Special School Gymnastics" after the Second World War (Cwierdzin-ski 2003). With the beginning of the 1980s, the term was replaced by "remedial teaching in PE" parallel to the development of psychomotor skills. The **goal of remdial teaching in PE** "is to teach children with special support needs by specially trained teachers" (Tiemann and Hofmann 2010, p. 106). In addition to regular classes, these additional educational offers should contribute to the pre-vention and **compensation of physical performance weaknesses** as well as motor, psychomotor, and psychosocial abnormalities. Based on a biomedical understanding, it is important to recognize the causes of physical inactivity in order to break the vicious cycle of "inactivity—functional underload—decrease in organ performance—increased inactivity" (Rusch and Weineck 2007, p. 30).

This functional argument is embedded in a deficit perception of children growing up in modern societies (e.g., Dordel 2007, pp. 26–42), which originates from a cultural pessimistic attitude (Neuber 2020, pp. 35–38). Nevertheless, the approach offers opportunities for individual support of adolescents. Physical education teachers with an **additional qualification** in remedial teaching in PE "have been extensively prepared for individual promotion during their training. They have the necessary diagnostic knowledge, can plan and evaluate a support measure, and are trained to deal with heterogeneity" (Kurth and Klein 2017, 75). Exercises and game forms are usually offered in **small groups**. To this end, teachers should create a trusting atmosphere in which children and adolescents "feel accepted with their wishes and weaknesses" (Kurth and Klein 2017, p. 72). In terms of compensating for deficits, the concept is usually **deductive-closed** in its methodological approach, but more open approaches are also possible during game phases. Newer approaches within the framework of inclusive school sports discuss renaming sports promotion education, for example, to "Joint Teaching".

The second sports-related concept is **talent support in sports.** A sports tal-ent is "understood as a person who is still in the early stages of development towards their individual peak performance and who is attributed the potential for the future development of particularly high performances and successes in top-level sports" (Güllich 2022, p. 766). Starting from the potential that a talent brings (talent factors), **athletic excellence** develops in specific, narrowly defined fields (excellence areas) through a process of dealing with environmental factors as well as with non-cognitive and non-somatic personality traits (Seidel 2011) (see Fig. 7.1). This form of talent promotion refers to the standardized, Olympic sports. The subject matter is therefore narrow and the teaching reference is usually deductive-closed. At least in individual sports, work is also done in small groups. Newer approaches go beyond this narrow sports talent concept and highlight the special potential of **movement talents** in non-Olympic fields, such as unicycling or movement theater, as well as **social talents,** such as sports assistents or referees (Pfitzner and Neuber 2020).

In contrast to other subjects, talent promotion in sports is not one of the tasks of the school. The responsibility for **performance and top-level sports** lies with the sports clubs and associations, which are independent in their actions from the state (Krüger 2019, pp. 194–198). Against the backdrop of the federal basic structure of organized sports, this has led to more or less complex **support systems for competitive sports** with "Sports Emphasized Schools", "Elite Schools of Sports" or "Partner Schools of Competitive Sports" (Güllich, 2022). The schools are usually only supposed to ensure a good compatibility of school and competitive sports. So far, little attention has been paid to the opportunities of school sports for **talent identification and promotion**. The guiding principle of individual promotion certainly includes starting points for a sports-related talent promotion in school (Bohn et al. 2010, pp. 296–297). The **all-day school** also offers opportunities for competitive sports promotion, which have so far been hardly used, although individual promotion is one of the core ideas of the all-day school (Kielblock et al. 2020). In addition, the school could also become active in the sense of the extended talent concept and specifically promote movement talents or social talents.

7.3.2   Individual Support through Sports

An initial concept for support *through* sports is the **learning promotion through movement.** Connections between movement and learning have long been known. As early as the beginning of the 1980s, for example, a study demonstrated the effect of movement offers on the intelligence development of preschool children (Zimmer 1981). Connections between physical activity and school learning have also been frequently established. Thus, **learning therapeutic approaches** assume that school learning disorders, e.g., reading-spelling or arithmetic weaknesses, can be treated through targeted movement exercises (Matthes 2009). However,

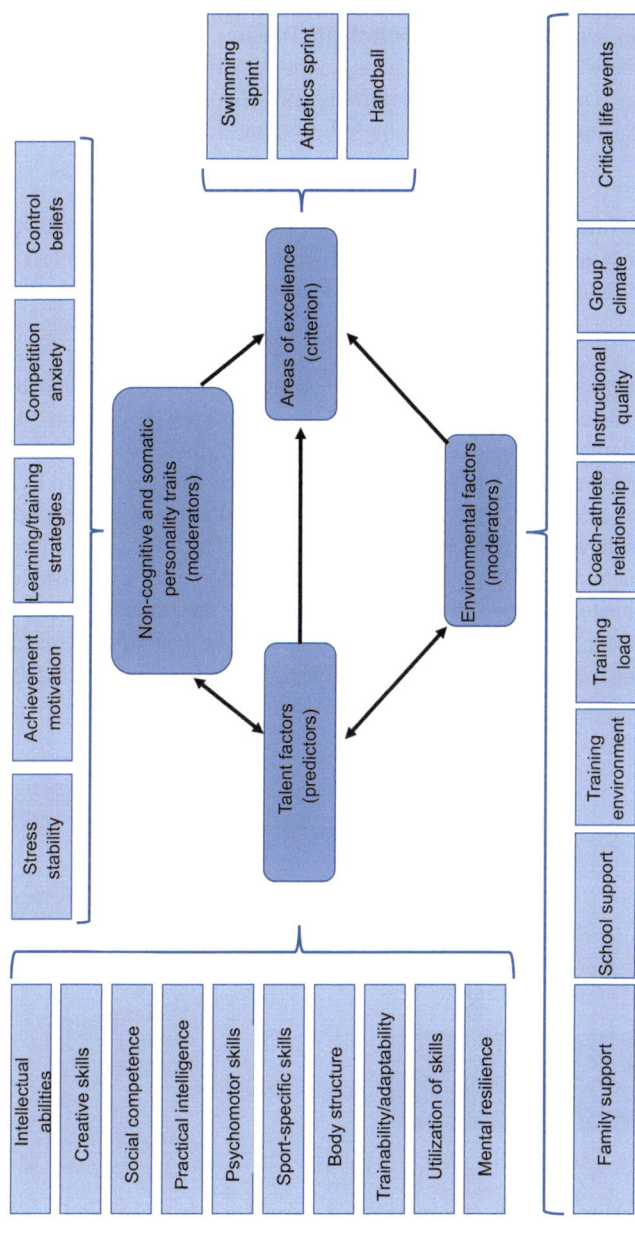

Fig. 7.1 Model of athletic talent. (Mod. according to Seidel 2011, adapted according to Hohmann 2009)

the effects of learning therapeutic interventions are hardly scientifically proven. It is different with **neurophysiological approaches**. Numerous studies prove correlations between motor activities, e.g., coordinative tasks or endurance performances, and cognitive aspects of learning and school performance. In this context, executive functions are increasingly becoming the focus of interest (Boriss 2015).

▶ **Executive functions** are cognitive control processes that are always required when cognitive automatisms are no longer sufficient for mastering a task. These include in particular working memory, inhibitory ability, and cognitive flexibility (see Fig. 7.2).

Executive functions are attributed a key function for the relationship between movement and learning. On the one hand, they can be well promoted through movement (Barenberg et al. 2011), on the other hand, there is a high correlation between executive functions and school performance (Best et al. 2011). Meanwhile, several studies are also available in the **school context**, i.e., the approach has been transferred from the laboratory to practice. The offer aims at promoting executive functions through movement and sports offers with cognitive demands and thus ultimately at the **self-regulation ability** of the students. Methodologically, the concept is rather closed-deductive, with the cognitive demand being able to be increased each time (Pfitzner and Eckenbach 2017; Pfitzner et al.

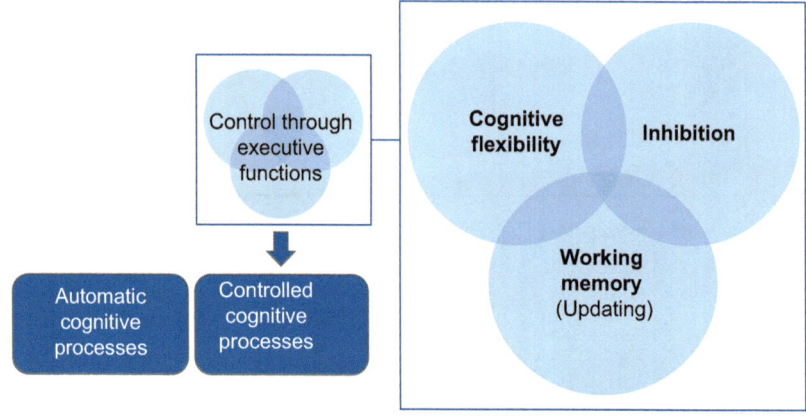

Fig. 7.2 Executive functions of learning. (Mod. according to Eckenbach 2017, p. 14)

2021). In addition, the tasks can not only be offered in physical education, but also in **classroom teaching** (Eckenbach and Ludwig 2021). Ultimately, this also overcame the deficient learning therapeutic approach. The concept thus aims at the individual promotion of all students. In this sense, "Learning and Movement" has now become an important topic of school sports development (Neuber 2017).

▶ **Literature tip** Eckenbach, K. (2017). *Games for Brains—Spielerische Lernförderung durch Bewegung*. Seelze: Kallmeyer.
Based on current research results, Karin Eckenbach presents numerous practical examples for promoting executive functions through movement, games, and sports in her book.

A second approach to individual promotion through movement is the concept of **psychomotor development support.** It is explicitly competence-oriented and assumes a close interlocking of psychological and physical processes (see Sect. 5.3.2). Movement action is understood as developmental action (Fischer 2019). Essential reference points of psychomotor development promotion are **perception and movement.** The guiding idea of psychomotor skills is the development of a harmonious personality through movement and play (Zimmer 2019). This means that the teaching of athletic skills takes a back seat: "Here, it is more about the child who, through movement, gets the opportunity to test themselves, to experience their body, to recognize their abilities and to further develop them" (Zimmer 1996, p. 75). For this purpose, psychomotor skills work with both open movement landscapes and guided movement offers that rely on the children's self-activity. From a methodological point of view, an **open-inductive approach** is pursued, which is understood as help for self-help in the sense of Montessori pedagogy (Neuber 2020, p. 42). Classic moto-therapeutic measures are rather offered in small groups, psychomotor offers in school, on the other hand, are rather offered for the entire class.

Psychomotor approaches exist today for all age groups up to old age (Köckenberger 2003). However, in school sports, the concept is mainly used in primary education. Psychomotor development promotion offers good starting points in terms of individual promotion because it addresses the **self-activity of the children** in dealing with encountered movement tasks or game arrangements (Zimmer 2019). In this context, psychomotor development promotion primarily focuses on the competencies of the children. However, psychomotor skills are less about promoting academic learning and more about a **child-centered development promotion** in the sense of a positive identity development (Zimmer 2019, p. 44). Thus, it also forms a bridge to the school sports discourse on development promotion through movement, games, and sports.

Development Support in Physical Education
The concept of development support originally comes from therapeutic and special education and entered the sports pedagogical debate about
an educational sports instruction through psychomotor skills (Neuber
2007, p. 18–22). Early on, Dietrich and Landau (1990) designed a **devel-
opment-oriented sports pedagogy,** which was based on a combination
of developmental psychology and socialization theory approaches. Prohl
(1999) developed the concept of a **movement education as development
support,** which is based on an interlocking of individual and environmental development factors. The course of development is understood as highly
individual, yet it includes general developmental tasks. The approach of a
movement-centered development support by Funke-Wieneke (2004)
concludes that "the developmental reference should primarily be sought in
movement development from a professional point of view and not be lifted
from the outset to general development promotion" (Funke-Wieneke (2004,
p. 172). General promotion can at best take place indirectly, through the
promotion of movement development.

Newer concepts, however, pick up the figure of the developmental
task again. Thus, the approach of **development support in adolescence**
relates the developmental task to concepts of pedagogical youth research.
The question is what specific contribution movement, games, and sports
can make to coping with subjectively and objectively significant developmental tasks in adolescence (Neuber 2007). The concept of the **developmental task** stands for the specific demands of an individual in the tension
field of psychophysical prerequisites, sociocultural requirements, as well
as individual goals and values, which have to be mastered in the transition
from one life stage to the next (see Fig. 7.3). In this overarching sense, the
development support through movement, games, and sports has been
one side of the dual mandate for school sports since the 2000 curriculum
reform in North-Rhine Westphalia. The pedagogical action of PE teachers
aims at the self-design capability of the individual in the sense of formation
("Bildung") (Beckers 2001). Why the term development support was chosen for this can ultimately no longer be clarified. However, development
support, like the concept of development itself, is now one of the established sports pedagogical terms (Neuber and Scheid 2021).

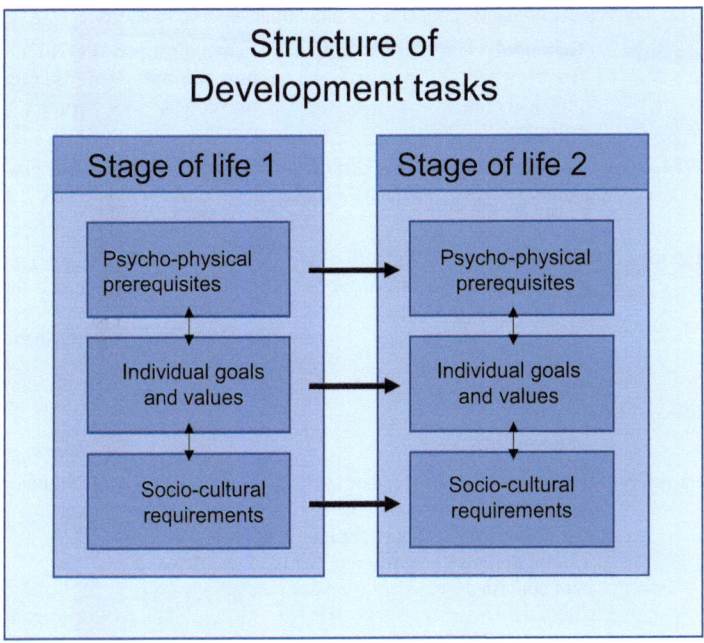

Fig. 7.3 Structure of developmental tasks. (Mod. according to Neuber 2007, p. 56)

7.4 Overview of Individual Support

Individual support has developed within a few years into an approach with far-reaching influence in the **educational discussion**. The idea of supporting each child and adolescent according to their individual abilities and talents, thereby unfolding their potential to the best possible extent, has found its way into the school laws of the states (e.g., MSB NRW 2022) and now influences school practice on many levels (Fischer et al. 2017). For school sports, individual support, in addition to educational PE, offers an **integrative concept,** that combines subject-specific and cross-curricular learning in sports and is also compatible with the general educational debate. Furthermore, current discourses on dealing with heterogeneity, such as special educational support or inclusive talent support, can be integrated into this approach (Neuber and Pfitzner 2021). If one combines the various conceptual approaches, a matrix emerges that differentiates between an **individual support** *of* and *through* movement, games, and sports on the one hand,

Table 7.2 Overview of didactic concepts for individual support in sports

	Remedial teaching in physical education	Talent support in sports	Learning support through movement	Psychomotor development support
Representative	Siegrid Dordel Andrea Kurth	Arne Güllich Michael Pfitzner	Karin Eckenbach Nils Neuber	Klaus Fischer Renate Zimmer
Guiding idea	Compensation of motor performance weaknesses as well as psychomotor and psychosocial abnormalities	Support of talents in sports	Support of executive functions of learning	Development support through perception and movement
Subject reference	Exercises and game forms for the compensation of deficits and abnormalities	Standardized competitive sports, open movement fields	Movement, games, and sports with cognitive demand	Movement and play
Teaching reference	Closed-deductive; small group work	Closed-deductive or open-inductive depending on orientation	Closed-deductive with potential for increase	Open-inductive; help for self-help

and a deficit- or competence-oriented approach on the other hand (Table 7.1). The four exemplarily selected didactic concepts can be compared (Table 7.2).

The **remedial teaching in physical education** aims at compensating for motor performance weaknesses as well as psychomotor and psychosocial abnormalities (Dordel 2007). To this end, it uses exercise and game forms to compensate for these deficits. Methodologically, the approach mostly works in a closed-deductive manner in small groups. The **talent support in sports** supports athletic talents on their way to peak performance within the framework of the association's competition system (Güllich 2022). In terms of content, it deals with standardized competitive sports and is accordingly taught in a deductive-closed manner in small groups. Newer approaches also refer to general movement talents and social talents (Pfitzner and Neuber 2020).

The **learning support through movement** originally stemmed from learning difficulties and tried to treat them therapeutically. Today, the approach primarily aims at self-regulation ability by promoting executive functions through movement and sports offers with cognitive demands (Pfitzner et al. 2021). Methodologically, work is usually done in a closed-deductive manner with increasing cognitive demands. The **psychomotor developmental support** aims at support through perception and movement and uses open and guided movement and game offers for this purpose (Zimmer 2019). The methodological approach is open-inductive in the sense of self-help.

The overview of the selected didactic concepts shows, on the one hand, the **content and methodological breadth** of individual support in PE. On the other hand, it becomes clear that not all approaches are suitable for school in their original form, mainly because they often work with small learning groups. Therefore, specific methodological considerations are necessary for application in the school context. The sports didactic **method discussion** is characterized by two polarizing approaches: On the one hand, there are approaches that are predominantly oriented towards the matter "sports" and proceed accordingly in a deductive-analytical manner. On the other hand, there are approaches that are oriented towards the "subject"; these approaches are more inductively-holistically oriented (see Chap. 6). This dichotomous juxtaposition can be differentiated by the **methodological dimensions** of Terhart (2019) with regard to individual support in PE. Thus, the dimension "framing" in school stipulates that usually one teacher is responsible for about 30 students. The dimension "target achievement" defines standard rules for all learners in the sense of competence-oriented curricula, so that individual goal settings are not easy to agree on (Pfitzner and Neuber 2012b, pp. 79–85).

Individual support in school sports is therefore only possible if there are didactic-methodological adjustments. This requires differentiation and individualization in particular. The **differentiation** in physical education is one of the central methodological measures for heterogeneous learning groups, with the focus essentially on internal differentiation, i.e., differentiation within a learning group. **Internal differentiation** can be defined with Heymann (2010, p. 7) as a collective term for all didactic, methodological and organizational measures that can be taken in class within a school class […] to better meet the diversity of students […] than in a predominantly synchronous, tendentially 'uniformizing' teaching". For the systematization of internal differentiation measures in teaching, Heymann (2010, pp. 8–9) suggests a consideration on a continuum between "open" and "closed measures" (see Fig. 7.4).

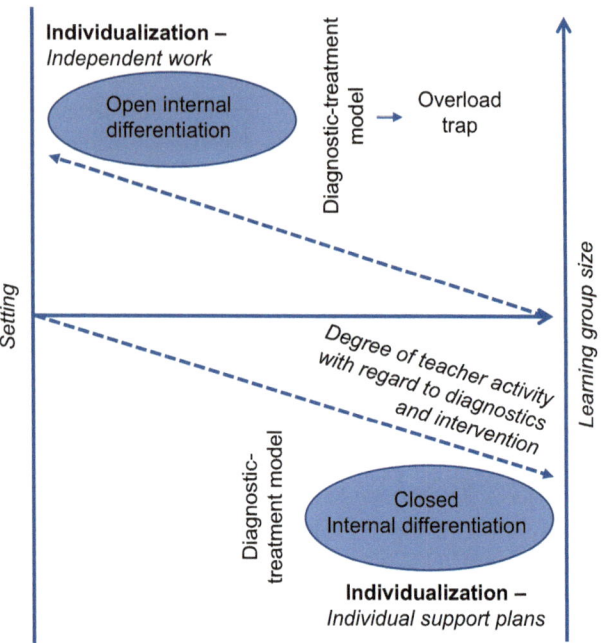

Fig. 7.4 Individualization of teaching. (Mod. according to Heymann 2010, pp. 8–9)

Closed internal differentiation measures are those in which the teacher assigns each student their learning path based on an individual diagnosis. Although this achieves a high level of individualization, it can only be used in specific settings, e.g. in learning therapy. In such a one-to-one situation, the "treatment-diagnosis model" applies, which can quickly lead to an "overload trap" for teachers in school (Heymann 2010). **Open internal differentiations** bypass the overload trap by providing their students with learning arrangements that they can use independently, that accompany and support the learners on their individual learning paths and give them differentiated feedback. The **individualization** of teaching requires learning offers from which the students can choose according to individual preferences, determine the sequence of work steps individually and increasingly control processes of relearning, practicing and repeating (Pfitzner and Neuber 2012b, p. 86–92). On this basis, **didactic recommendations** can be derived, for example for the training of learners' methodological competence, for the learning support of teachers or for a changed role of the learners, who must take responsibility for their own learning process (Pfitzner and Neuber 2012a).

Reflection Questions

1. Why is individual support a characteristic of good teaching?
2. To what extent are both teachers and learners equally challenged for the success of individual support?
3. What is understood by pedagogical diagnostics?
4. How is individual support related to the idea of potential orientation?
5. Why is the concept of individual support an integrative concept for school sports?
6. How do concepts of individual support *of* sport differ from concepts of individual support *through* sport?
7. What forms of talent support exist in sports?
8. Why is "learning and movement" an important topic for school sports development?
9. Why can't all concepts of individual support in sports be applied in physical education?
10. How do closed and open forms of internal differentiation differ?

References

Arnold, K.-H., Graumann, O., & Rakhkochkine, A. (2008). *Handbuch Förderung – Grundlagen, Bereiche und Methoden der individuellen Förderung von Schülern.* Weinheim, Basel: Beltz.

Barenberg, J., Berse, T., & Dutke, S. (2011). Executive functions in learning processes: Do they benefit from physical activity? *Educational Research Review, 6*(3), 208–222.

Beckers, E. (2001). Sportpädagogik und Erziehungswissenschaft. In H. Haag & A. Hummel (Eds.), *Handbuch Sportpädagogik* (pp. 25–33). Schorndorf: Hofmann.

Best, J. R., Miller, P. H., & Naglieri, J. A. (2011). Relations between executive function and academic achievement from ages 5 to 17 in a aarge, representative national sample. *Learning and Individual Differences, 21*(4), 327–336.

Bohn, C., Brach, M., Krüger, M., & Pfitzner, M. (2010). Der Beitrag des Sportunterrichtes zur Talenterkennung im Kontext individueller Förderung. *Sportunterricht, 59, 297–301.*

Boriss, K. (2015). *Lernen und Bewegung im Kontext der individuellen Förderung – Förderung exekutiver Funktionen in der Sekundarstufe I.* Wiesbaden: Springer VS.

Brezinka, W. (1990). *Grundbegriffe der Erziehungswissenschaft – Analyse, Kritik, Vorschläge* (5., verbesserte Aufl.). München, Basel: Reinhardt.

Cwierdzinski, P. (2003). Sportförderunterricht aktuell. Das Stiefkind des Schulsports? *Sportpädagogik, 27*(3), 44–47.

Dietrich, K., & Landau, G. (1990). *Sportpädagogik,* Reinbek: Rowohlt.

Dordel, S. (2007). *Bewegungsförderung in der Schule. Handbuch des Sportförderunterrichts* (5. edn.). Dortmund: Modernes Lernen.

Eckenbach, K. (2017). *Games for Brains – Spielerische Lernförderung durch Bewegung.* Seelze: Kallmeyer.

Eckenbach, K., & Ludwig, K. (2021). *KlassenSpiele: Classroom Games for Superbrains. Lernförderung durch Bewegungspausen.* Hannover: Kallmeyer.

Eckert, E. (2016). Individuelles Fördern. In H. Meyer (Eds.), *Was ist guter Unterricht?* (15. edn., pp. 86–103). Berlin: Cornelsen.

Fischer, C. (2014). *Individuelle Förderung als schulische Herausforderung.* Berlin: Friedrich-Ebert-Stiftung.

Fischer, C., Fischer-Ontrup, C., Käpnick, F., Mönks, F.-J., Neuber, N., & Solzbacher, C. (Eds.). (2017). *Potenzialentwicklung. Begabungsförderung. Bildung der Vielfalt. Beiträge aus der Begabungsförderung* (Begabungsförderung: Individuelle Förderung und Inklusive Bildung, 4). Münster: Waxmann.

Fischer, C., & Fischer-Ontrup, C. (2020). Diagnosebasierte Individuelle Begabungsförderung und Talententwicklung. In C. Fischer, C. Fischer-Ontrup, F. Käpnick, N. Neuber, C. Solzbacher & P. Zwitserlood (Eds.), *Begabungsförderung, Leistungsentwicklung, Bildungsgerechtigkeit – für alle! Beiträge aus der Begabungsforschung* (pp. 223–239). Münster, New York: Waxmann.

Fischer, K. (2019). *Einführung in die Psychomotorik* (4., überarbeitete und erweiterte Aufl.). München: Reinhardt.

Funke-Wieneke, J. (2004). *Bewegungs- und Sportpädagogik: Wissenschaftstheoretische grundlagenzentrale Ansätze – entwicklungspädagogische Konzeption* (Bewegungspädagogik, 1). Hohengehren: Schneider.

Graumann, O. (2008). Förderung und Heterogenität – Die Perspektive der Schulpädagogik. In K.-H. Arnold, O. Graumann & A. Rakhkochkine (Eds.), *Handbuch Förderung – Grundlagen, Bereiche und Methoden der individuellen Förderung von Schülern* (pp. 16–25). Weinheim, Basel: Beltz.

Güllich, A. (2022). Talente im Sport. In A. Güllich & M. Krüger (Eds.), *Sport – Das Lehrbuch für das Sportstudium* (2. edn., pp. 761–796). Berlin: Springer Spektrum.

Hanke, P. (2010). Einleitung. In P. Hanke, G. Möwes-Butschko, A. K. Hein, D. Berntzen & A. Thieltges (Eds.), *Anspruchsvolles Fördern in der Grundschule* (pp. 1–8). Münster: ZfL.

Helmke, A. (2003). *Unterrichtsqualität erfassen, bewerten, verbessern.* Seelze: Kallmeyer.

Helsper, W. (2010). Pädagogisches Handeln in den Antinomien der Moderne. In H.-H. Krüger & W. Helsper (Eds.), *Einführung in Grundbegriffe und Grundfragen der Erziehungswissenschaft* (9. edn., pp. 15–34). Wiesbaden: VS.

Heymann, H. (2010). Binnendifferenzierung – eine Utopie? Pädagogischer Anspruch, didaktisches Handwerk, Realisierungschancen. *Pädagogik, 62*(11), 6–11.

Hohmann, A. (2009). *Entwicklung sportlicher Talente an sportbetonten Schulen. Schwimmen, Leichtathletik, Handball.* Petersberg: Imhof.

Ingenkamp, K., & Lissmann, U. (2008). *Lehrbuch der pädagogischen Diagnostik* (8. edn.). Weinheim, Basel: Beltz.

Kielblock, S., Arnoldt, B, Fischer, N., Gaiser, J. M., & Holtappels, G. (Eds.). (2020). *Individuelle Förderung an Ganztagsschulen – Forschungsergebnisse der Studie zur Entwicklung von Ganztagsschulen (StEG).* Weinheim, Basel: Juventa.

Knauder, H., & Reisinger, C.-M. (2017). Aspekte des Verständnisses von individueller Förderung seitens der Lehrerinnen und Lehrer an Grundschulen – Eine quantitative Inhaltsanalyse. In H. Knauder & C.-M. Reisinger (Eds.), *Individuelle Förderung im Unterricht – Empirische Befunde und Hinweise für die Praxis* (pp. 11–24). Münster: Waxmann.

Köckenberger, H. (Eds.). (2003). *Psychomotorik – Ansätze und Arbeitsfelder.* Dortmund: Modernes Lernen.

Krüger, M. (2019). *Einführung in die Sportpädagogik* (4., neubearbeitete und aktualisierte Aufl.). Schorndorf: Hofmann.

Kunze, I. (2016). Begründungen und Problembereiche individueller Förderung in der Schule – Vorüberlegungen zu einer empirischen Untersuchung. In I. Kunze & C. Solzbacher (Eds.), *Individuelle Förderung in der Sekundarstufe I und II* (5., aktualisierte Aufl., pp. 15–32). Hohengehren: Schneider.

Kunze, I., & Solzbacher, C. (Eds.). (2016). *Individuelle Förderung in der Sekundarstufe I und II* (5., aktualisierte Aufl.). Hohengehren: Schneider.

Kurth, A., & Klein, D. (2017). Sportförderunterricht aktuell – zwischen Inklusion und individueller Förderung. *Sportunterricht, 66,* 71–76.

Laging, R. (2017). *Bewegung in Schule und Unterricht – Anregungen für eine bewegungsorientierte Schulentwicklung.* Stuttgart: Kohlhammer.

Matthes, G. (2009). *Individuelle Lernförderung bei Lernstörungen – Verknüpfung von Diagnostik, Förderplanung und Unterstützung des Lernens.* Stuttgart: Kohlhammer.

MSB NRW (Ministerium für Schule und Bildung NRW). (2022). *Schulgesetz für das Land Nordrhein-Westfalen.* Abgerufen am 29.12.2022 unter: https://www.schulministerium. nrw/schulgesetz-fuer-das-land-nordrhein-westfalen.

Neuber, N. (2007). *Entwicklungsförderung im Jugendalter – Theoretische Grundlagen und empirische Befunde aus sportpädagogischer Perspektive* (Wissenschaftliche Schriftenreihe des Deutschen Olympischen Sportbundes, 35). Schorndorf: Hofmann.

Neuber, N. (2017). Bildung und Bewegung – Zum Zusammenhang von Lernen und Bewegung in der Schule. In C. Fischer, C. Fischer-Ontrup, F. Käpnick, F.-J. Mönks, N. Neuber & C. Solzbacher (Eds.), *Potenzialentwicklung. Begabungsförderung. Bildung der Vielfalt. Beiträge aus der Begabungsforschung* (pp. 105–118). Münster: Waxmann.

Neuber, N. (2020). *Fachdidaktische Konzepte Sport – Zielgruppen und Voraussetzungen* (Basiswissen Lernen im Sport). Wiesbaden: Springer VS. https://doi.org/https://doi. org/10.1007/978-3-658-28464-0.

Neuber, N., & Pfitzner, M. (Eds.). (2012). *Individuelle Förderung im Sport – Pädagogische Grundlagen und didaktisch-methodische Konzepte* (Begabungsforschung, 14). Münster: Lit.

Neuber, N., & Pfitzner, M. (2021). Inklusive Begabungsförderung im Sport. In C. J. Kiso & S. Fränkel (Eds.), *Inklusive Begabungsförderung in den Fachdidaktiken – Diskurse, Forschungslinien und Praxisbeispiele* (pp. 96–110). Bad Heilbrunn: Klinkhardt.

Neuber, N., & Scheid, V. (2021). Entwicklungstheoretische Ansätze. In E. Balz, S. Reuker, V. Scheid & R. Sygusch (Eds.), *Sportpädagogik – Eine Grundlegung* (pp. 77–89). Stuttgart: Kohlhammer.

Oefner, J., Erlemeyer, R., & Staack, A. (2009). *Fördern und Fordern – Diagnostik und individuelle Förderung im Sportunterricht der Sekundarstufen I und II.* Arnsberg: Bezirksregierung.

Pfitzner, M., & Eckenbach, K. (2017). Bewegung und Lernen – Förderung exekutiver Funktionen in der Schulpraxis. In C. Fischer, C. Fischer-Ontrup, F. Käpnick, F.-J. Mönks, N. Neuber & C. Solzbacher (Eds.), *Potenzialentwicklung. Begabungsförderung. Bildung der Vielfalt – Beiträge aus der Begabungsforschung* (pp. 137–148). Münster: Waxmann.

Pfitzner, M., & Neuber, N. (2012a). Individuelle Förderung – Fachdidaktische Konzepte, Bedingungen und didaktische Empfehlungen. *Sportpädagogik, 35*(5), 2–8.

Pfitzner, M., & Neuber, N. (2012b). Individuelle Förderung im Sport – Didaktisch-methodische Grundlagen. In N. Neuber & M. Pfitzner (Eds.), *Individuelle Förderung im Sport – Pädagogische Grundlagen und didaktisch-methodische Konzepte* (pp. 75–95). Münster: Lit.

Pfitzner, M., & Neuber, N. (2020). Talente im Sport – Neue Perspektiven zur leistungssportlichen Förderung junger Athletinnen und Athleten. In C. Fischer, C. Fischer-Ontrup, F. Käpnick, N. Neuber, C. Solzbacher & P. Zwitserlood, P. (Eds.), *Begabungsförderung, Leistungsentwicklung, Bildungsgerechtigkeit – für alle! Beiträge aus der Begabungsförderung* (pp. 155–173). Münster: Waxmann.

Pfitzner, M., Neuber, N., Eckenbach, K., Liersch, J., Ludwig, K., & Aschebrock, K. (2021). Lernförderung durch Bewegung – Die Auswirkungen von Bewegung auf das exekutive System und Potenziale für einen lernförderlichen Sportunterricht. *Sportpädagogik, 45*(1), 2–8.

Prohl, R. (1999). *Grundriß der Sportpädagogik.* Wiebelsheim: Limpert.

Rusch, H., & Weineck, J. (2007). *Sportförderunterricht – Lehr- und Übungsbuch zur Förderung der Gesundheit durch Bewegung* (6., überarbeitete und erweiterte Aufl.). Schorndorf: Hofmann.

Schrader, F.-W. (1989). *Diagnostische Kompetenzen von Lehrern und ihre Bedeutung für die Gestaltung und Effektivität des Unterrichts.* Frankfurt: Lang.

Schrader, F.-W., & Helmke, A. (2001). Alltägliche Leistungsbeurteilung durch Lehrer. In F. E. Weinert (Eds.), *Leistungsmessungen in Schulen* (pp. 45–58). Weinheim, Basel: Beltz.

Seidel, I. (2011). Trends in der Talentforschung und Talentförderung. *Leistungssport* (2), 19–23.

Terhart, E. (2019). *Didaktik – Eine Einführung.* Stuttgart: Reclam.

Tiemann, H., & Hofmann, A. R. (2010). Vom Sportförderunterricht zum Sportunterricht in inklusiven Settings. In H. Lange & S. Sinning (Eds.), *Handbuch Methoden im Sport* (pp. 107–116). Balingen: Spitta.

Zierer, K. (2021). *Ein Jahr zum Vergessen – Wie wir die Bildungskatastrophe nach Corona verhindern.* Freiburg: Herder.

Zimmer, R. (1981). *Motorik und Persönlichkeitsentwicklung bei Kindern im Vorschulalter.* Schorndorf: Hofmann.

Zimmer, R. (1996). Psychomotorik in der Grundschule. In M. Polzin (Eds.), *Bewegung, Spiel und Sport in der Grundschule – Fachliche und fächerübergreifende Orientierung* (S. 70–81). Frankfurt: AK Grundschule.

Zimmer, R. (2019). *Handbuch Psychomotorik – Theorie und Praxis der psychomotorischen Förderung von Kindern* (14. edn.). Freiburg: Herder.